ED MONK AND THE *TRADITION* OF *CLASSIC BOATS*

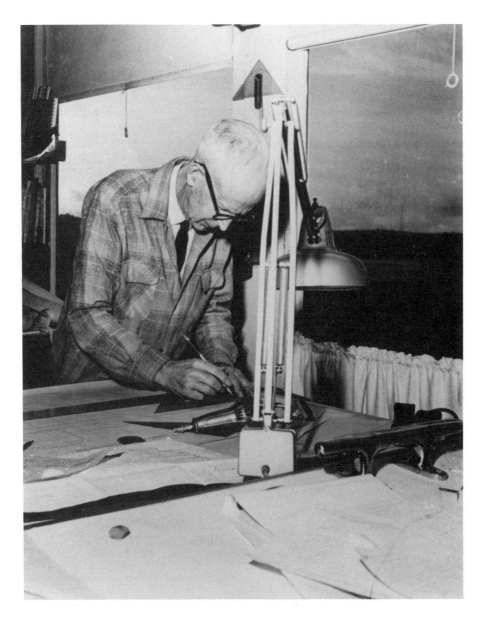

Ed Monk. (Gordon Jones, courtesy of Ed Monk Jr.)

ED MONK AND THE TRADITION OF CLASSIC BOATS

BET OLIVER

HORSDAL & SCHUBART

Horsdal & Schubart Publishers Ltd., Victoria, B.C., Canada

Front cover photographs: centre: *Netha*, courtesy of Eric Finn; clockwise, from above
left: *Wood Duck*, Bruce Kenning, courtesy of Ian Kenning; *Grand Finale*, courtesy of Larry
and Colleen Price; *Holiday*, courtesy of Dan Bartlett; *Solander Isle*, courtesy of Lee
Morris; *Rita*, courtesy of Lew and Lindy Barrett; *Halcyon II*, courtesy of Harry Stamhuis.
Back cover photographs: Ed Monk, courtesy of Judy Wade; *Nan*, courtesy of Diane
Anderson; Bet Oliver, courtesy of Alan Oliver; *Longboard*, courtesy of Bet Oliver.

This book is set in Lapidary 333 Book Text.

We acknowledge the support of the Canada Council for the Arts for our publishing
program. We also wish to acknowledge the financial support of the Government of
Canada through the Book Publishing Industry Development Program (BPIDP) for our
publishing activities. We also acknowledge the financial support of the Province of
British Columbia, through the British Columbia Arts Council.

Printed and bound in Canada by Printcrafters, Inc., Winnipeg, Manitoba.

National Library of Canada cataloguing in publication data

Oliver, Bet, 1953-
Ed Monk and the tradition of classic boats

Includes bibliographical references and index.
ISBN 0-920663-59-1(cloth)—ISBN 0-920663-60-5 (paper)

1. Monk, Edwin. 2. Naval architects—Washington (State)—Seattle—Biography.
4. Boats and boating—Northwest, Pacific. I. Title.
VM140.M68044 1998   623.8'2'0092   C98-910110-X

Printed and bound in Canada

CONTENTS

In Memory of Jerry Dick, 1928 - 1998
Sailor, aviator, fisherman, friend.

ACKNOWLEDGMENTS

BOOKS SUCH AS this one are not so much written as assembled, a testimony to the goodwill and generosity of contributors who shared their knowledge, precious memories and photographs.

Paul Helman, son of Ed Monk's eldest daughter, Josephine Helman, devoted many years to researching his family background, collecting memoirs, newspaper and magazine articles, and photographs, which he made available at the beginning of this project. He answered countless questions, with an appreciation for detail yet always keeping in mind the way that Ed Monk's career fit into the larger context of maritime history. Without Paul's support and encouragement, this would have been a much slighter book.

Judy Wade contributed photographs and delightful remembrances of her mother, Ann Monk. In addition, Judy put me in touch with her nephew, Paul Helman, and her aunt, Isabel Van Valey, who wrote fondly about *Ann Saunders* and *Nan.*

Ed Monk Jr. took time from a busy schedule to provide invaluable plans and photographs, and to explain technical and historical aspects of boat design. His love for his work — combined with his insight and expertise — make him a natural storyteller, and a privilege to interview.

Donna Shields, coordinator of the Seattle-based Ed Monk Wooden Boat Club, welcomed me aboard *Topaz*, little knowing that she would soon be spending hours tracking down boats. Donna and her husband, Ken Shields, remained unflaggingly cheerful and hospitable during our long year of gathering information for the book. Thanks also to Seattle photographer Dave Ellis, who donated his time and skill making copies of U.S. Monk Club photographs.

Fred Bailey sent articles about the Grandy Boat Company, along with rare photographs, and Oscar Lind sent articles from *Pacific Motor Boat.* Addy McRae loaned plans, as did Arthur Rendell, and

Fred Stolzenberg displayed his exquisite models. Rob Morris at *WestCoast Mariner* and Gloria Kruzner at *Nor'westing* passed along important addresses.

There are not many people in the northwest more interesting to listen to than those who have spent their lives building boats: George McQueen, Henry Clark, Tolly Tollefson, Jim Dryburgh, and Earl Wakefield, to name but a few. George McQueen and Henry Clark graciously consented to interviews in their homes; I met with Tolly Tollefson aboard *Tolly*, and Jim Dryburgh aboard *Three Martlets*. Earl and Dora Wakefield came to visit me from Port Angeles, bringing wonderful stories, photographs, and common-sense advice. Norman Blanchard, Phil Barron, and Robert Benson spoke with me by telephone.

Robert Osborne shared years of knowledge about boating during our meeting aboard *Rao*. Laurie and Bonnie Derrien, Warren Heard, and Roy Parkinson patiently took me through boats they had built, from wheelhouse to engine room. John and Mary Ann Beveridge, Cameron Elder and Rich Karvonen, Gerry Flowers, Jim Genge, Ian and Margaret Kenning, Michael Knight, William Ovalle and Robert Peck, Arthur and Heather Rendell, Peter Smith, and Warren Whyte — all provided tours of their boats.

Perhaps because of my lack of a fax machine, an e-mail address, and even an answering machine, or perhaps because many contributors predated the electronic era, I received beautifully written letters in response to my queries. A heartfelt thank you to Emslie "Bim" Clark, Doug Egan, Hugh Garrett, John Guzzwell, Tom Kincaid, Harry Runer, and Robert Gibson, whose *Gibson Gal*s have graced the coast since the 1950s. Thanks also to Richard Asia, Rosie Atkinson, Jo Bailey, John Bailey, Lew and Lindy Barrett, Dan and Tami Bartlett, Steve Bradford, Mike and Gwen Byrne, Eric Finn, George and Betty Hansen, J. Ellsworth Jensen, Tom and Mary Bess Kelly, Jeanette Lucrisia, Dan and Barb Moldenhauer, Carl and Barbara Montford, Kaare Norgaard, Bob and Marci Plank, Larry and Colleen Price, Don Sandall, James Shanahan, Richard and Darlene Smith, Bill Szabo, and Cyril Thames. Canadian Monk Wooden Boat Club members who helped out included Claude and Diane Bigler, Jim Brass, Elmer "Buck" Buckingham, Bob Cross, Morley Forsyth, Hugh and Lisa Gordon, Steve and Susi Jorgensen, John King, Len and Lorraine Klinger, Susan MacDonald, Mike Michalson, Wayne and Chris Robinson,

Graham Ross-Smith, John Seeland, Harry Stamhuis, Mike and Barb Stone, Bill and Judith Waddell, Dougall and Erma Warren, Gordon and Darlene Weir, Chris and Sue Wilson. Gordon Nickells volunteered an entire album of photographs of *Bendora*, and Maurice Green spoke with me by telephone. John West provided information on *Scaup*, and Diane Anderson rounded out *Nan's* story with anecdotes and photographs. Vic Griffin educated me on marine engine development, and Norm Collins contributed an entertaining account of his decades on the water. R. L. Stewart was a lively correspondent on many subjects, not the least being the 80 boats he has owned over the past 50 years.

Tracking down the workboats was an even greater challenge than the yachts, and I am indebted to Ron Kondrat for his detailed letters, suggestions, and magazine articles. Doug Barron led me to *Solander Isle*, whose skipper, Don Bostrum, shared his experiences fishing off Vancouver Island's west coast; Lee Morris assisted with updated information and photographs. Bill Osborne described the early years of building fishing boats, and Pete Peterson provided information on *Miss Pacific*. Vern Sampson wrote eloquently about *Hookline No. 3*, as did John Parkyn about *Bonnie Belle*.

In addition to the contributors mentioned above, there were others — historians and librarians — who supplied reference materials. *Yachting* and *Pacific Motor Boat* deserve credit for the articles they published by and about Ed Monk, beginning in the early 1930s. My apologies to anyone I have inadvertently omitted, and also for any errors in the book.

My husband, Alan Oliver, and I learned to sail on Jerry Dick's Hobie Cat off Tofino, B.C., in 1975. Our first home was a 40-foot ketch, which we rebuilt; then we owned a succession of runabouts used for camping in the Gulf Islands with our two sons, David and James. Our passion for exploring the west coast led us three years ago to *Longboard* (formerly *Aqua-Knot II*), a 42-foot heavy duty cruiser built by West Bay Boat Builders of Delta, B.C., in 1968. *Longboard* has provided us with many opportunities to appreciate the fine qualities of a Monk design.

Lastly, my thanks to my editor, Marlyn Horsdal, and particularly to Michael Schubart — without whose vision this book would remain a mere wish among all of us who cherish classic boats.

Bet Oliver, February 1998

INTRODUCTION

WALKING THE DOCKS or gazing across any harbour in the Pacific Northwest, one is sure to hear, "Look, there's a Monk boat." Or, even more emphatically, "That *must* be a Monk." From skiff to salmon troller, sailboat to classic yacht, Ed Monk produced more than 3,000 designs during his 46 years as a naval architect.

While this book recognizes the work of numerous boatbuilders, many other highly reputable yards have been building Monk boats since the 1930s. It should be understood that this is by no means a complete history of Ed Monk's designs; for every boat mentioned, there were hundreds more not described. Ideally, one would have infinite time and resources to document boats and builders, and I regret those missed. Several boats which are included are derivations of Monk designs, and are noted as such. Although I have striven for accuracy, information was lost during changes in boat ownership, and not every detail could be double-checked.

Readers will notice discrepancies in spelling. Words such as "center/centre," "harbor/harbour" were spelled according to their source, reflecting standard American and Canadian use.

Ed Monk drew boats, built boats, wrote about boats and, in the words of those who knew him, understood boats, pioneering many innovations which are commonplace today. His designs are renowned for their efficiency, their strength, and their pleasing lines. Many styles have come and gone through the decades, but a Monk boat brings lasting satisfaction to the eye. His contribution to naval architecture is recognized by colleagues, builders, and owners who have taken their boats safely across all the world's seas.

CHAPTER ONE

FOUR GENERATIONS OF SHIPWRIGHTS

ED MONK WAS born on January 1, 1894, at Port Blakely, Bainbridge Island, Washington. He was named George Edwin William after his father, George Monk, a prominent Puget Sound shipwright. The Monk family had come to America from Plymouth, England, where Ed Monk's grandfather and great-grandfather built ships for the British navy.

On the wall of Ed Monk's Seattle, Washington, office was a copy of the document which had indentured his great-grandfather, John Monk, to Joseph and William Moore's Shipyard in Plymouth, an apprenticeship which began in 1814 and lasted seven years, paying five shillings a week. John Monk's son, also called John, went on to have seven children, one of whom, George Richard Emmet, born in 1845, became Ed's father.

George learned the family trade and, like many young men of the time, began looking overseas to the colonies for challenging work. Around 1863 George and his brother, Elijah, left England for Australia, sailing on the famous clipper ship *Red Jacket*. They found employment in Brisbane but were soon enticed by the United States, where the California gold rush had created a demand for shipwrights. Elijah, who by now had a wife and child, booked passage on the modern, steel-hulled *Coya*, while George travelled aboard an older, slower vessel. The *Coya* strayed off course as it approached the California coast, hitting a reef near Santa Cruz on November 20, 1866; none of the passengers survived.

George Monk reached Puget Sound, Washington Territory, in late 1866. His first job was at Hall Brothers in Port Ludlow, constructing the schooner *Annie Gee*. The hull was formed with the ship's "curves" he had brought from England, made out of holly and pear wood. He later passed these curves on to his son, Ed, who used them for many years. When Ed

Monk had new curves made out of plastic, they were shaped to the precise dimensions of those that his father had carried across two seas.

Hall Brothers moved to Port Blakely in 1880, and George Monk became general superintendent of the yard. The flurry of activity around the gold rush had been replaced by steadier commissions from the cod-fishing fleet and the lumber industry, and George worked six days a week, earning three or four dollars a day. During his 26 years at Hall Brothers he supervised the construction of more than 90 schooners, barkentines, tugboats, revenue cutters, and motor auxiliaries.

In 1893 George married Ann Saunders and together they raised five children: Edwin, Arthur, Geoffrey, Edith and Jesse. Despite long days at the shipyard, George came home to build skiffs and sailing dinghies with his sons. He purchased several properties, including a large farm beside the Green River in Kent, Washington. In 1900 he moved to the farm and began working at Robert Moran's shipyard in Seattle, where the battleship *Nebraska* was being built. The Monk children attended school in Kent; they were a close and happy family.

When Ed Monk graduated from Kent High School in 1914, his father was on Orcas Island building Robert Moran's three-masted schooner, the *San Juan*. Ed Monk apprenticed to Robert Moran, helping his father complete the 130-foot yacht, during which time the shipwrights lived at Moran's island estate.

With the onset of World War I, the Monk farm at Kent was leased out and the family moved to Seattle. In 1915 George took his sons Ed and Arthur to St. Helen's, Oregon, to work on *The City Of Portland*, one of the largest freighters ever built of wood, a technical challenge for even the most experienced shipwrights. With so many steel vessels requisitioned for the war, causing a serious shortfall in cargo transport, the federal government offered financing for the construction of more wood freighters. Two Seattle businessmen, Meacham and Babcock, set up a yard at Salmon Bay, the future site of the Fishermen's Terminal. They asked George Monk to become the general superintendent, using his reputation to help secure a contract to build 12 ships.

George was 72 years old, and his health was failing after a lifetime of hard work. Nevertheless, the country was in a state of emergency and he took the job with Meacham and Babcock, hiring his son Ed as superintendent of hull construction. In May 1918, the yard launched the *Bolton*, their first ship.

Earlier, Ed Monk had spent his days off at the family's summer home in Redondo, Washington. Here he met his future wife, Blossom Bradford,

The Monk family, around 1896. George, Edwin, Arthur, Anna and little Edith. (COURTESY OF PAUL HELMAN)

who worked at the Redondo General Store. Blossom was the daughter of a local shipwright, which may have been good preparation for her courtship with Ed, much of it spent in his canoe. One of Ed's gifts to Blossom was a hope chest he built out of scraps of Port Orford cedar at St. Helen's. The chest was later passed on to their eldest daughter, Josephine, then to Josephine's son, Paul Helman, who gave it to his wife, Nancy, as a wedding present.

Although Ed Monk was turning out to be a skillful shipwright, he decided that he was more interested in designing than in building, a decision supported by his father, who presented him with his first set of drafting tools. He attended evening classes in drafting at Broadway High School and studied his father's books on design. By the time the *Bolton* was launched, Ed had become engaged to Blossom, and the entire yard at Meacham and Babcock, 1,400 employees, turned out for their wedding celebrations. The September 1918 issue of the *Shipyard News* reported on the fund set up by the employees in appreciation of Ed, to help him get "under way." Blossom was given a bouquet of flowers and one more little present, for emergency use — a rolling pin!

Midway through 1919, George Monk suffered a stroke. When it became apparent that he could not continue as general superintendent, he was replaced by his son. The last of the 12 ships was launched in October 1919, and Meacham and Babcock shut down. In December, George Monk died.

Ed Monk found work at several different shipyards in the Seattle area, studying naval architecture by correspondence. He was entering a field dominated by west-coast designers such as Edson Schock, Joe Fellows, Hugh Angelman, Thomas Halliday and L. E. Geary, all of whom attracted national attention throughout the early part of the century. In 1925 Monk applied to the Blanchard Boat Company, which had just moved from a shop south of Seattle to Lake Union and had been growing steadily since its founding by Norman C. Blanchard in 1905. During the mid-1920s the company was building motor cruisers in the "Dreamboat" style, a name copyrighted by the Lake Union Construction and Dry Dock Company. Monk was hired as a shipwright, and was given his first opportunity to try his hand at small-boat design.

Norman C. Blanchard's son, Norman J., was 14 years old when Ed Monk first showed up at the shop. Seventy years later, Norman J. recalled how they had become friends. "Not only did he willingly let me use his tools to make my toy boats, he would sharpen them for me." [1] Norman J. Blanchard took over the company after his father died, going on to build many of Monk's designs.

Ed Monk with his father, George, at Redondo Beach, Washington, around 1918. (COURTESY OF PAUL HELMAN)

Photo taken for Ed Monk's employment at Meacham & Babcock, 1918. (COURTESY OF PAUL HELMAN)

FORM NO. 6

C. G. HEIFNER, RECEIVER FOR

MEACHAM & BABCOCK SHIPBUILDING COMPANY

FIFTEENTH AVENUE WEST AND EMERSON STREET

SEATTLE

YARD LOCATION:
SALMON BAY, NEAR BALLARD

October 18, 1919

Mr. E. G. Monk
Seattle

My dear Mr. Monk:

The launching of the Charnis today, which completes the building of twelve hulls in this yard, and completes our contract with the United States government, for the construction of twelve ships of 3500 tons capacity, makes it necessary to close these yards, and necessitates the severance of your connection with this company. I sincerely regret the necessity which compels this separation and I take this occasion to say that you have been connected with this company since the beginning of its work for the government, acting as assistant to your father, G. R. E. Monk, who was superintendent of hull construction up to July 1, 1919. Since that date you have been our superintendent of construction and have launched our two last ships. I am glad to testify to your ability and efficiency, both in the matter of handling men and in the construction of hulls, and the best recommendation that I can give you is to say that in my own judgment, you are a worthy son of a sire, who may justly be called illustrious in the shipbuilding line.

Yours very truly,

MEACHAM & BABCOCK SHIPBUILDING COMPANY

By

Receiver

CGH.RDD

Monk's letter of recommendation from Meacham & Babcock. (COURTESY OF PAUL HELMAN)

One of the naval architects working with the Blanchard Boat Company was L. E. "Ted" Geary. Along with his previous partners, Lloyd and Dean Johnson, Norman C. Blanchard had built the Geary-designed *Helori*, a 100-foot motor yacht, and the champion racing sloop *Sir Tom*. Although *Sir Tom* was owned by a syndicate of Seattle businessmen, Ted Geary was often at the helm, bringing trophies home from all over the coast. His design practice was thriving, and in 1926 he offered Monk a job for $50 a week. "It was a godsend to Geary," recalled Norman J. Blanchard. "Ed Monk was an excellent draftsman, and he knew the inside of a boat." [2]

Ed Monk knew boats well enough by then to build one for himself, *Ann Saunders*, with the help of his brother Art. This was the first of ten power cruisers designed by Monk for his own use over the next five decades. He and his wife had been living at the family farm in Kent when their first child, Josephine, was born in March 1921. A second daughter, Isabel, arrived in May 1923.

In her memoirs, Josephine, later Jo (Monk) Helman, described those early years. "My father and my Uncle Art were trying their hand at dairy farming at that time. Dairy farming proved disastrous for my father — the herd became infected with disease and had to be destroyed, and dad went broke. After a few years of working in the shipyards, he became associated with L. E. Geary and we moved to Seattle. I always felt I had a very unique childhood because of my father and boats. He built a 32-foot boat in the backyard, the *Ann Saunders*, named after my paternal grandmother. I recall the steam box he built, that he would fire up and steam planks so that they could be bent to fit on the ribs and keel to shape the boat. I remember the day it was trucked from our backyard to the water — what an event for the neighborhood in 1926." [3]

The family was living on 22nd Avenue North in Seattle, and the launching marked the beginning of their boating life. "We spent many happy hours and weekends on the *Ann Saunders*," recalled Isabel, later Isabel (Monk) Van Valey. "We had no automobile then so transportation to and from the boat was by streetcar, taking all the food and clothes." [4] Like the popular "Dreamboats," *Ann Saunders* was a raised-deck trunk-cabin cruiser, with a 25 hp, four cylinder Fordson tractor engine converted to marine use. In 1929 she was sold to Larry Peterson of Seattle, her owner for the next 33 years. The Fordson engine had been replaced by a Chrysler Ace when she was bought in the early 1960s by Ken and Donna Shields, who kept her for 14 years.

When Ed Monk went to work for him, Ted Geary was well known for his fast, stylish yachts described as express cruisers, used by wealthy busi-

above: Ann Saunders, *Ed Monk's first boat.* (COURTESY OF PAUL HELMAN)

below: Ann Saunders, *owned during the 1960s by Ken and Donna Shields, Bainbridge Island, Washington.* (COURTESY OF DONNA SHIELDS)

"My sister and I, we were five and three at the time, were tied to a ring in the stern of the cockpit. I remember my mother braiding the ropes in the backyard and fixing the harness. The ropes were long enough for us to go anyplace in the boat. It was the only way she could have peace of mind while out on the water. I hated this rope and recall people feeling sorry for us and commenting about 'those poor little girls being tied' as we would go through the locks, so I would sit on the rope to hide it from the people. I don't remember at what point I didn't have to be tied but eventually I was assigned to either the bow or stern of the *Ann Saunders* to help with the ropes or lines when we would go through the locks.

"We often went to Winslow or Port Madison or nearby protected bays. One special memory comes to mind — we were anchored in Winslow — my father commuted to work in Seattle on the passenger steamer, in fact he stayed in Seattle overnight. The wind came up one night and we were adrift in the dark. I wonder what my mother was thinking, alone in the boat with two small girls? In the harbor was an old sailing boat, the *Conqueror*, and living aboard was Captain Hershey. He and his wife were caretakers. He became aware of our trouble and tied us to his ship. Our families became friends and stayed in touch for many years." Jo (Monk) Helman. [1]

nessmen commuting throughout Puget Sound. Geary had just finished supervising the construction of fifteen 75-foot rum chasers, and it had been rumoured that several of his high-speed launches ended up in the California-to-Canada rumrunner trade, although they were not intended for that purpose. These were "the father of today's fast cruiser," according to Monk. [5] Geary was also much in demand for commercial projects: sturdy vessels to service northern British Columbia and Alaska canneries; forestry patrol boats such as the 50-foot *Ranger VIII*; and *Bluefin*, an 86-foot patrol and research vessel for the California fish and game commissioner.

Local shipyards were busy; in addition to contracts such as these, they serviced the fishing fleet and the lumber-carrying schooners and barkentines. Smaller shops like the Blanchard Boat Company and the Grandy Boat Company were setting a new trend with the stock production of high-quality cruisers for families to enjoy in Puget Sound.

The Seattle-based *Pacific Motor Boat* magazine had been started in 1908, as "The Journal of Recreational and Commercial Boating on the Pacific." The magazine featured many plans by Geary, "attracting much favorable comment in Northwest boating circles as well as California." [6] Typical of Geary's designs was the 52-foot stock cruiser built by the Lake Union Construction and Dry Dock Company in 1929, outfitted with a 175 hp two-to-one reduction gear Hall-Scott motor, capable of 16 knots. The hull was double-planked red cedar, the superstructure was teak, and the galley contained a Kelvinator ice machine, automatic fresh-water service pump, Oxo kerosene burner, and running hot and cold water. The plush seating, full-height wardrobes, and colour-coordinated heads reflected Geary's elegant standards for the times.

Monk contributed information on Geary's work to *Pacific Motor Boat*, becoming close friends with the editor, Daniel Pratt. The first Monk design to appear in print was an 11-foot sailing dinghy, in 1928. Monk went on to publish many articles over the years, writing in a warm, forthright style which simplified his designs and made them appealing to "the man of moderate means." [7]

In 1928 the Seattle Yacht Club asked Ted Geary to design a fast, safe class of day sailers, following the tragic drowning of four young racers on Lake Washington. Their Star boat, its watertight bulkheads unsecured, had swamped and sunk. Geary came up with the "Flattie," an 18-foot planing centreboarder, and young Norman J. Blanchard, apprenticed to his father, was given the job of building the first ten boats. Monk produced plans for a similar but smaller class racer, the 12-foot, six-inch "Truant," and many

Ed Monk, around 1928. (COURTESY OF PAUL HELMAN)

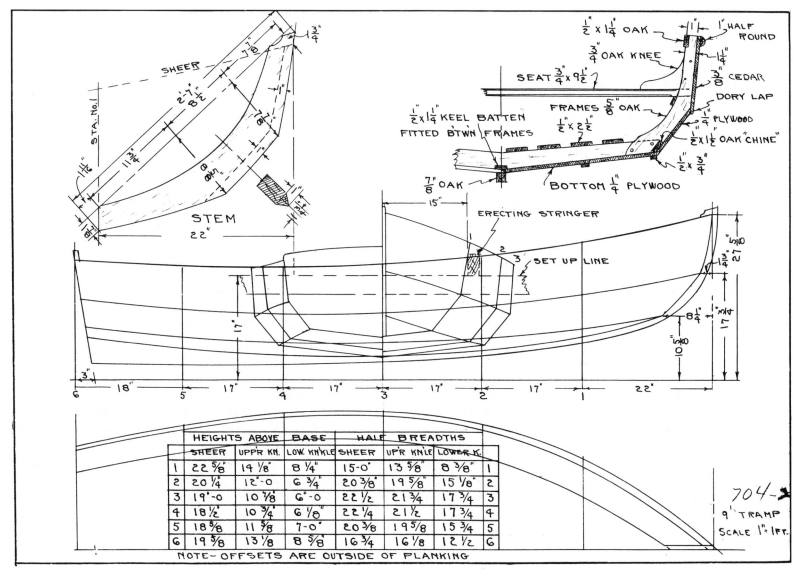

Plan No. 704, 9-foot "Tramp." Monk published a variety of dinghy designs in *Pacific Motor Boat.* *"A simple little pram dinghy,"* he wrote, *"... will be a good winter's job for the boat owner in need of a new dinghy, or anyone desiring a light, safe, and seaworthy little rowboat."* Instructions called for six-penny nails and pieces of burlap or blankets soaked in boiling hot water to bend the bilge planks. *"Will carry four adults,"* he added reassuringly, *"with plenty of freeboard to spare."* [2] (COURTESY OF ED MONK JR.)

other designs from Geary's office during the late 1920s and early 1930s were drawn by Monk.

Growth in the boating industry came to a halt in 1929, when the stock market crashed. The west-coast ports fell quiet in the worldwide depression that followed; the stately fleet of cargo schooners that Ed Monk's father had worked on lay deteriorating at anchor. A few companies kept their doors open, saved by their less expensive stock cruisers, but many yards went out of business. In October 1930, Ted Geary decided to move to Long Beach, California, to be closer to his wealthy Hollywood clients. Monk went with him, joined later by his young family who travelled by steamship from Seattle.

Geary was working on his first steel design, *Infanta*, a luxurious, 120-foot cruiser for John Barrymore. Launched in 1930 at the Long Beach yards of the Craig Shipbuilding Company, *Infanta* was powered by twin 275 hp, six cylinder Atlas Imperial diesel engines and cost around $200,000. *Infanta* had teak decks, a three-quarter-ton ice machine, a cruising range of 7,000 miles, and a smoking room "furnished in the nautical style of Seventeenth Century Mariners." [8] Barrymore, who loved to fish, also commissioned Geary to design a fast, 22-foot tender with upholstered swivel seats. *Infanta* was bought by the Foss tug and barge family of Washington in 1950, and renamed *Thea Foss*.

Even though he was "assistant naval architect attached to Ted Geary's office" [9] on these extravagant projects, Monk was developing his own approach to his work. "He was a very reserved sort of person, quiet and unassuming," said Seattle maritime historian Doug Egan, who had known Monk since 1925. [10] He was shaped not only by the economic mood of the country but also by the modest, traditional values of a father who had supported and encouraged his talents. "My father was a great one for self-help," Monk said. [11] The challenge was to come up with efficient designs "to create the best boat, the appropriate sized boat for the least money for the most people." [12] Yachting magazines began featuring his detailed "how-to" articles, such as the one for a 30-foot express cruiser which could be turned out by the average shop for $3,250. The cabin sides could be curtained in bad weather, "but don't forget, however, this adds weight, a mighty important item in a fast boat .... The builder must keep in mind that lightness is a first consideration. Speed is more than anything

else a product of weight and horsepower, so do not increase the scantlings shown." [13] In 1931 he designed the 30-foot *Maydo*, based on the lines of an Atlantic Coast sea skiff and outfitted with a 106 hp Chrysler marine engine. Tested by stopwatch on Lake Washington, *Maydo* reached a top speed of 20 mph.

Monk wrote about his ideas on all aspects of boating, from stowing dinghies to the use of emergency sails on power cruisers. Although sails had been discarded as engines became more reliable, he recommended a small, loose-footed jib, and thought that most boats could be sailed provided they had some keel and normal beam, and were not too top-heavy. His suggestion for outriggers installed off a vessel's stern — for "the sometimes bothersome dinghy" [14] — listed advantages which exemplified his practical approach: 1) one man could handle the job; 2) the boat is always ready to launch in a hurry; 3) no boat cover to take off; 4) there is a better chance of successful launching in rough weather; and 5) it is a time saver.

Even more importantly, Monk was encouraging the frugal boating public, and the backyard builder, to trust an expert's advice. "There are ways and means of dodging your architect, but, like dodging the law, is it worthwhile?" A prospective owner might have limited funds, say $4,000 to spend, of which seven percent would go to the architect, "for plans, specifications, a little inspection, and a lot of conversation." But this amount would buy an extra item for the boat, perhaps an electric anchor winch, and the owner might decide to ask a friend, who has some talent, to draw up the lines. The contract will lack many essentials, Monk cautioned, and the boat will probably be a disappointment. Owners sometimes try to incorporate their own ideas and make changes without consulting the designer, the worst offenders turning out to be those building from plans published in boating magazines. "Slight changes in arrangement are, of course, of no consequence, but when large weights are shifted and hull lines altered, trouble is sure to follow." His description of the unfinished vessel "which still stands like the skeleton of some prehistoric monster, weatherbeaten and neglected, some day to make firewood, but never a boat" must surely have left his readers suitably forewarned. [15]

For those with lesser ambitions, Monk suggested building a half-model, an appropriate ornament for any home or office,

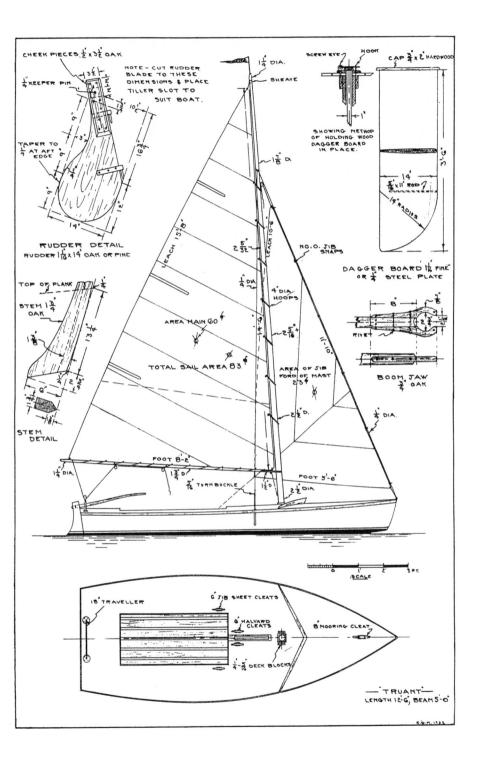

The 12½-foot "Truant." "A Simplified Sailer ... practically nonsink-able and can be built at the absolute zero in cash expenditure." [3]

because "most of us cherish the lines of a boat." His instructions made the project seem as uncomplicated as the tools: "a chisel, a gouge, and of most importance, a good spokeshave. Clamps are useful in gluing up but, as they are not generally available, a few dozen wood screws will do the trick." [16]

With the depression came lowered construction costs; the average boat-builder's wage had dropped by more than half. "Why a Better Time To Build?" Monk titled one of his articles, in 1933. Local sawmills had closed down or were running at reduced capacity, converting stockpiled wood into much-needed cash at a great sacrifice, " a condition that will of course not continue." [17] It was the motor that would give the most savings: one leading manufacturer of marine engines had just announced a price cut in all models of 30% to 40%.

A further blow to pleasure boating had been narrowly averted in 1932, when the proposed ten percent sales tax for all boats built and sold was replaced, after much lobbying, with a sliding user's tax. Boats with a length over 28 feet and under 50 feet paid ten dollars, and the tax was in place for only two years. Even so, with low wages and few jobs, these were years in which considerable resourcefulness was required by anyone starting out on a new career.

Ed and Blossom Monk and their daughters, Josephine and Isabel, around 1932. (Courtesy of Paul Helman)

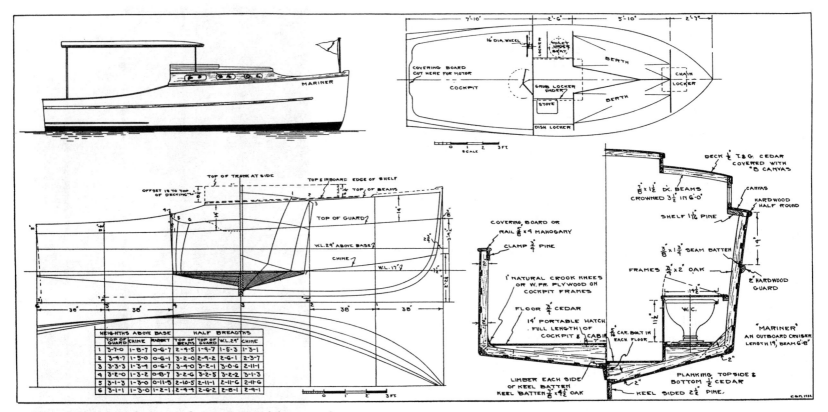

"Mariner," length 19 ft., beam 6 ft. 8 in. "...intended as a complete
little cruiser for two or three, and contains a large cockpit, berths,
galley, and toilet, which, after all, is the nucleus of any yacht." [4]

CHAPTER TWO

A CAREER BEGINS

IN 1933 MONK'S employment with Ted Geary ended when he returned to Washington, though he continued his association with Geary, acting as "representative" for his designs. "My father decided to go into business for himself," recalled Jo (Monk) Helman, "so after two years at Long Beach we moved back to Washington. He built a trailer and we moved all our worldly goods in it. The day we arrived at my grandmother's place in Thomas was the day of the terrible Long Beach earthquake." [1]

When Jo was about 11, the family moved to the Monk summer home at Redondo, Washington. They had $3,500 in savings and Ed Monk designed a 50-foot boat for himself, Plan No. 1, marking the beginning of his independent career. Once again, his brother Arthur came to help with the building. Monk's son, Ed Monk Jr., remembered his father describing how he and Arthur bought an entire railroad car load of vertical grain, old-growth fir for $25, but they had to unload it themselves. Shortly after the boat was finished, Arthur got a job on the United States Coast and Geodetic Survey, which had been formed to upgrade coastal navigation charts and provide information about tides, currents, and hazards. He became the ship's carpenter on the survey vessel *Pathfinder* and worked for many years along the Alaska coast, retiring from the Survey in 1955.

The new boat was called *Nan*, the nickname of Monk's mother, Ann. The hull was double-planked with red cedar, and they installed a 40 hp, four cylinder Lathrop gas engine, which was hand-started using a bar. *Nan* became both a family home and floating office, Monk's solution to making a living and taking care of his wife and children in uncertain times.

Monk's eldest daughter, Josephine, was given the honour of swinging the bottle at the christening, and the launching date was set for May 30, 1934, which was Isabel's birthday. Family members arrived, and the road in front

Ed Monk, right, and his brother, Arthur, around 1932.
(COURTESY OF PAUL HELMAN)

of the home was closed so that the ways to guide the boat to the water could be built. Paul Helman, Monk's grandson, described the launching, from his mother's journal account: "High tide at 3:00 pm was the selected time to knock out the chocks and send the *Nan* down the ways. The excitement began to build as the water rose. Ed's mother, Ann, watched proudly as the Monk family tradition of shipwrights continued. Ed's brother-in-law, John Green, was selected to ride *Nan* into the water. Arthur had the hammer to hit out the chocks. As the appointed time approached, the wind began to pick up. All eyes were on Ed as he stroked his chin and worried about the wind. Finally, the moment arrived, and he announced in his direct, efficient way, 'Not today, it's not safe, let's try tomorrow.' Disappointment was felt by all, many of whom would not be able to return to watch. Saddest of all was Isabel, who felt she had missed the best birthday present ever." [2]

Isabel and Josephine Monk, at the launching of Nan, *1934.* (COURTESY OF PAUL HELMAN)

"With that $3,500 [their savings], for which you couldn't get a good engine today, we built the boat and paid our living expenses aboard her for almost the first year," Monk recalled in 1962. "The office was about four-by-four and cramped all right, but it filled the bill in the circumstances. We moored at the Seattle Yacht Club most of those years until business picked up so I could establish an office on the downtown waterfront." [3]

Isabel described her father's office as a small cubbyhole in the corner of the pilothouse, just big enough for the drawing board, a client, and himself. That little corner was the only part of the boat which was changed, converted to a chart table, 60 years later when *Nan* was restored. Monk eventually sold the boat to his friend Art Russell, who kept *Nan* for about 18 years and loaned her to the navy during World War II, to patrol the waters of Puget Sound. *Nan* also participated in time-lap races, winning several runs from Olympia to Nanaimo, B.C. John and Jackie Bleakly purchased *Nan* from Art Russell's estate, then sold her in 1994 to Steve Hemry and Diane Anderson of Bothell, Washington, who completed her restoration.

Monk's first book, *Small Boat Building*, was published by Charles Scribner's Sons in 1934 and was an immediate success. Dedicated to the yachtsman who builds his own boat, the book contained advice on how "to produce a nice appearing design that in every way looks the part, but with simplicity of construction always kept in mind." [4] From "the lowly skiff" to the 17-foot keel sloop "Vagabond," Monk listed all the required steps and materials, even to the equipment on board: whistle, lights, and at least two copies of the Pilot Rules. He included plans for several outboard runabouts, a type which he recognized as becoming increasingly

above: Nan, *Plan No. 1.* (COURTESY OF PAUL HELMAN)

below: Doing chores on Nan *at the Seattle Yacht Club.* (COURTESY OF PAUL HELMAN)

"There are three of life's possessions that are almost indispensable, each entailing a major investment. These are a home, a car and a boat. The car is, in modern life, a necessity, the home also, and to give up the boat is almost unthinkable. So let us combine the home and the boat." Ed Monk. [5]

PHONE EAST 8548

EDWIN MONK
NAVAL ARCHITECT

Cruiser "NAN," 1807 Hamlin Street,
Seattle, Wash.,

"Note the phone number — the Seattle dock phone. When a client would call up, the phone would ring and ring until someone answered it ... imagine running a business that way today!" Paul Helman. [6]

left: Nan *in 1997, restored by liveaboards Steve Hemry and Diane Anderson. Diane invited Isabel and her nephews, including Paul Helman, to visit the boat, the first time Isabel had seen* Nan *since moving off as a teenager. "It was fun to watch her. She looked under the amidship steps to see if the storage bins were still there for her mother's canned goods. She sat here in the saloon and saw a pipe running up the port side by the steering, which was for the air horn. She remembered that it had been her job to blow the horn, so I went back to the shop and searched through the* Nan *stuff, and found the horn. I polished it up and it sounds great!" Diane Anderson.* [7] (COURTESY OF DIANE ANDERSON)

below: Blossom Monk's berth aboard Nan. (COURTESY OF DIANE ANDERSON)

above: Looking forward from Nan's *main cabin towards the galley in the bow.*
(COURTESY OF DIANE ANDERSON)

*below: Ed Monk's "cubbyhole" on the right, later converted to a chart table with the walls
removed. Isabel and Josephine used to stand behind their father, watching him work.*
(COURTESY OF DIANE ANDERSON)

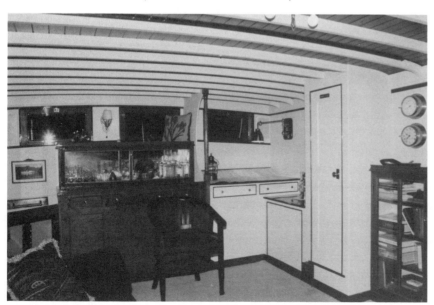

NAVAL ARCHITECTS AND YACHT BROKERS

Pacific Motor Boat, April 1935. (COURTESY OF PAUL HELMAN)

Pacific Motor Boat advertises Monk's new book.

popular, "fast, light, safe and dry boats, with freeboard and a generous flare forward." [5]

The economy began to show signs of improvement throughout 1934. The west-coast commercial fishing and cargo fleet was slowly rebuilding, and pleasure-boat industry sales had been given a boost by several major regattas. Santa Monica's new 2,000-foot breakwater created a safe haven for boaters, and membership in yacht clubs was growing every month. Sixty-five vessels participated in the 1934 International Cruiser Race from Seattle to Nanaimo, B.C. "The fact that only one out of the sixty-five failed to finish is a further tribute to the acumen of coast yachtsmen, the dependability of the modern marine engine, and the skill of west coast designers and builders." [6]

Monk's long and profitable association with the Grandy Boat Company was initiated in 1934 when the company announced his design for a 42-foot stock cruiser, to be completed in plenty of time for a spring delivery. The Grandy Boat Company, formed in the early 1920s by brothers Earl and Bill Grandy, was fast becoming one of the busiest yards on Lake Union. Their formula was simple: 16-hour days of expert craftsmanship. This resulted in a steady stream of commissions — from 12-foot lapstrake dinghies, numbering in the thousands, to stock production boats like the "Grandy 28" which decades later sold for three times its original price. Monk's new cruiser for Grandy was expected to cost $7,500, with sleeping accommodations for eight. The hull had a round bilge and generous flare forward, a 100 hp motor and a speed of 14 knots.

With his reputation outgrowing his cubbyhole on *Nan*, Monk set up an office ashore in 1935. The "Crow's Nest," a Seattle newspaper column, reported that he could now be found at 66 Marion Street, in the Maritime Building, a location more convenient for his clients. "He also designed the boatsheds behind the building," said Ed Monk Jr., "which is why they are tall enough to take some decent-sized spars on boats." [7] Monk bought a piece of property at Port Madison, Washington, which he and his young family visited aboard *Nan* on weekends. They cruised extensively through the San Juan Islands and the Gulf Islands, with relatives and friends. Monk's mother, Ann, had three sisters and a brother who lived Victoria, B.C., another frequent destination.

Monk was ideally situated to consider the needs of liveaboards: built-in dining nooks with windows low enough to see out of comfortably, galleys with good-sized sinks and ice boxes, adequate ventilation and lots of storage space. "Some of the nice things about living aboard are that the motor is always warm and dry and ready to start. You never have to worry

Ed Monk moved his office ashore, needing a little more space for his customers and his drawings. (COURTESY OF JUDY WADE)

(COURTESY OF PAUL HELMAN)

Log of the *Nan*, September 10, 1934: "Left for Spit for clams. Fished and dug clams. 1 cod, 1 sole, 3 rat fish, 2 dogfish. While Capt. and Mrs. was ashore dragged anchor about 1 mile. Windy." [8] (COURTESY OF PAUL HELMAN)

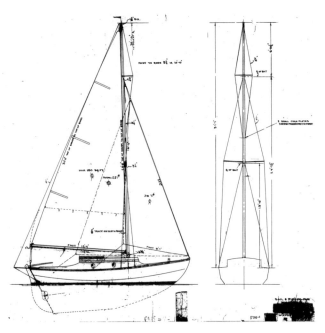

"Vagabond III," Plan No. 506, 21-foot sloop.
(COURTESY OF ED MONK JR.)

"Ed Monk's sailboats are universally beautiful, which is important, but almost never won any races, so the 'hot dog' sailors usually looked elsewhere for their designs. Perhaps my favorite anecdote about Ed Monk happened when I was in junior high school — probably about 13 years old, 60 years ago. A neighbor boy and I had started to build an 18-foot sailboat we found in a little book Ed Monk had written called *21 Boats And How To Build Them*. It was a beautiful little double chine sloop designed as a day sailer, with a couple of feet of the bow covered to stow your lunch.

"The other boy, Troxell Paris, and I decided we wanted to make this boat into a cruising boat so we could visit the San Juans and Gulf Islands. We had no trouble converting the centerboard into a fixed keel, ...

about freezing and, in fact, it starts more easily in winter than summer. There is no lawn to cut, but there is a lot of scrubbing and painting. In summer one can anchor away from the city and commute, in winter you are as snug as can be, with all the comforts of home. And the home problem and the boat problem become one problem and one care instead of two!" [8]

Monk's designs were achieving wider recognition: the Rodd brothers of Victoria, B.C., launched the 42-foot power cruiser *Dawn* in 1936. *Dawn* had a 115 hp, eight cylinder Lycoming gas engine, and made numerous trips to Alaska and around Vancouver Island. In 1996, *Dawn* was purchased for restoration by John Seeland of Ladysmith, B.C.

"Big Times Ahead," reported *Pacific Motor Boat*. "Naval architects up and down the coast claim they have more work in sight for next season than ever before at this time of the year and the same is true of the boat-builders. These are not just optimistic hopes but real orders." [9] Similar upswings were happening in the east, with Chris Craft, Matthews, Richardson and other stock boat builders claiming that 1936 was one of the best years in their history.

Despite the fact that it was his power boats that primarily paid the bills, Monk enjoyed drawing sailboats of all sizes and types, particularly admiring the work of English designer Uffa Fox. "There is much good cruising ground on this Pacific Coast that is not accessible to the deep draft keel boats, waters where a boat built for just such an environment would offer a great deal of cruising fun." His 20-foot "Ebb Tide" carried 230 square feet of sail and drew just 20 inches with the centreboard up. Even with the smallest projects, safety and seaworthiness were Monk's first considerations: the cockpit was watertight, and the hatches sealed. "She is a sturdy, staunch little ship with no frills but plenty of comfort .... A large sliding hatch provides headroom in the galley, there is sitting headroom on the two berths, and a real woodstove would make it comfortable in the coldest weather." [10] Plans could be obtained from *Pacific Motor Boat* for just $7.50 which included a year's subscription to the magazine.

Netha, a 45-foot marconi-rigged cutter, was built by William and Clarence Foss in Bremerton, in 1936. A year later her stern was extended, a modification also designed by Monk. *Netha's* hull was Alaska yellow cedar over oak frames; displacement was nine tons, with 6,400 pounds of cast iron in a full keel. After leaving the Foss family, *Netha* spent many years in the Tacoma Yacht Club with several owners, then was sold to Bill Langdon in the 1970s and kept at Shilshole Bay. She was bought by Eric Finn in 1996, and moored on the east shore of Lake Union.

Netha alongside the University of Washington boat barn, near the Montlake Cut. "Netha *is powered by the wind, and a Perkins four cylinder auxiliary diesel. She is a traditional cutter design featuring a single mast placed amidships rigged fore and aft, carrying a mainsail and two headsails. Her hull is deep and narrow with a raking transom stern, a vertical stem, and a long bowsprit. Her character is very typical of Monk-designed sailboats for the waters of Puget Sound during the '30s and '40s."* Eric Finn. [9] (COURTESY OF ERIC FINN)

Log of the *Nan*, July 18, 1936: "Major A.W. Johnson, wife, and son, Robert Milton Bradford, Miss Bonnie Lee Bradford and immediate family on trip to see launching of Clarence and Bill Foss's sailboat. Going from Port Madison around island to Colby. Saw launching of *Netha*, went in very nice. Came home around other side of B. [Bainbridge] Island, got there about 9:30." [10] (COURTESY OF PAUL HELMAN)

we simply cut a piece of boiler plate to the right shape, had a flange welded on, and bolted it onto the keel. But when it came to adding a trunk cabin, we ... were suddenly over our depth. Adding the cabin trunk meant we had to raise the boom, which was going to affect the sailing balance of the boat. Using what little we could learn about this problem, we carefully drew in the cabin on our plans, and then I made a trip to see Mr. Monk. This involved simply taking the streetcar downtown to the National Building on the waterfront and riding the elevator to the third floor where Mr. Monk had his office.

"The problem was that I was very shy, and had already canonized Ed Monk. I stood outside his door for quite a while before I got up the courage to knock. The door was answered by this tall (he wasn't, really, but to me he was nine feet tall) gentleman, dressed in a black suit. He invited me in and instantly put me at ease. He took the grubby plans from me and spread them out on one of two long drawing tables. He then spent the next couple of hours gently educating me about 'forces of lateral resistance' and 'centers of effort' of sails, as well as heeling forces and lateral planes. Meanwhile he was redoing my sail plan, drawing on a piece of parchment, explaining every step of the process.

"When he was finished, he handed his work to me and walked me to the door. 'Sail over to Port Madison when you finish that little boat,' he said. 'I'd like to go for a sail in it.' I've always regretted that I never did go for a sail with Ed Monk — that would have been a highlight of my life. The exigencies of amateur boat-building together with discovering girls slowed the process, and by the time we finished the boat World War II interfered. I've thought of Ed Monk as some sort of God ever since that day in his office. He was truly what is meant when you refer to someone as a 'gentleman.' " Tom Kincaid, founder, *Nor'westing* magazine. [11]

	HEIGHTS ABOVE BASE					HALF BREADTHS									DIAGONALS		
	UNDER RAIL	BOT. 18"	BUT. 9"	RABETT	KEEL BOT.	UNDER RAIL	W.L. 6'9"	W.L. 6'0"	W.L. 5'3"	W.L. 4'6"	W.L. 3'9"	W.L. 3'0"	W.L. 2'3"	KEEL BOT.	DIA.1	DIA.2	DIA.3
1	9-3-7	7-11-5	6-3-0	5-5-3	5-2-0	1-9-2	1-0-0	0-7-1	0-1-0						1-3-6	1-7-3	1
2	8-10-6	5-3-3	4-4-5	3-9-2	3-6-0	3-0-0	2-4-3	1-11-7	1-5-5	0-10-1	0-2-5	0-6-7	0-2-2	0-0-9			
3	8-6-7	9-0-0	3-2-6	2-9-1	2-2-2	3-10-3	3-5-4	3-1-7	2-8-2	2-0-2	1-2-2	0-6-7	0-2-2				
4	8-4-0	3-3-4	2-6-0	2-3-1	0-11-5	4-9-7	4-2-5	4-0-1	3-7-5	3-0-0	2-1-1	1-7					
5	8-2-1	3-0-5	2-3-2	2-0-6	0-3-3	4-7-6	4-7-3	4-5-7	4-2-4	3-7-2							
6	8-1-4	3-2-3	2-5-2	1-11-1	0-1-3	4-7-6	4-8-0	4-6-7	4-7-2								
7	8-0-7	3-8-4	3-1-6	2-0-0	5/8 BELOW	4-5-1	4-2										
8	8-0-2	4-6-9	4-1-6	3-4-5	2 3/4"	4-2											
9	8-1-2	5-7-1	5-4-1	5-2-2	5												
10	8-2-0																

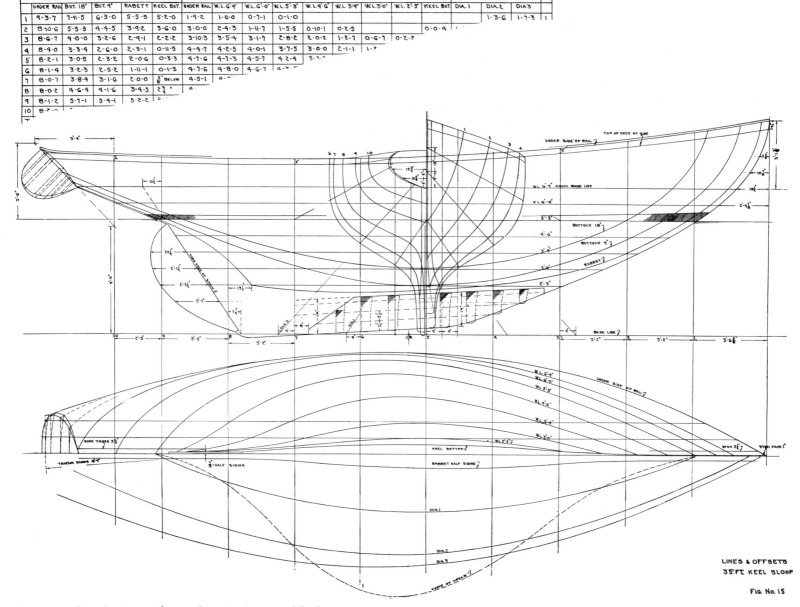

Lines and offsets for sloop Kiletan, *from Monk's second book,*
Modern Boat Building.

"I had built a Snipe sailboat and soon had other ideas. I was given a copy of Ed's book *Small Boat Building* at Christmas 1934. I quickly learned that Ed Monk and his family lived on the *Nan* located at the Seattle Yacht Club.

"I soon went to the *Nan* and introduced myself to Ed. Of course I did not realize it at the time but that was the real start of a wonderful life of boats for me. Ed was a wonderful man to talk to. He was a superb listener. I told him of my desire of a bit larger boat that I could build in my back yard. He told me that at the time he was designing some small boats to be written up in the *Pacific Motor Boat* magazine. The next boat to be designed for the magazine was a 21-foot sailboat that he thought would suit my needs very well.

"He not only sold me the plans for a very reasonable price but the advice and help he gave me couldn't be bought. I worked long and hard at building that boat but, looking back, I'd never have been able to accomplish what I did without Ed's help.

"Like most boat nuts I soon wanted a larger boat as by that time I crewed on other larger ones. Of course I went to Ed and told him of my dreams. As usual he was interested and designed a 34 foot 6 inch sloop. Amateur that I was, I had just about finished laying down the lines when Ed came up with the idea that the newly commissioned Boat School might want to build a boat like that. He did all the consulting and they agreed to build it. Jim Chambers was the instructor at that time and no finer boatbuilder in the country could be found than Mr. Chambers.

"We named the boat *Kiletan* (arrow in Chinook). Lived on it for some months while at the Queen City Yacht Club. I raced the boat and often Ed was my navigator.

"I find it difficult to write of Edwin Monk without overdoing it ... he was probably the finest gentleman that I ever met. In all my associations with him I never saw him lose his temper or get excited. Never heard him say an unkind word of anyone. He seemed to like PEOPLE and to want to see them enjoy themselves on boats which he loved. I've talked to many boatbuilders and they all agree, Ed never drew anything in a set of plans that couldn't be put there. There are very few people who, when leaving this world, leave such a legacy of appreciation for their good works as Edwin Monk." Hugh Garrett. [12]

Watauga, *sister ship to* Kiletan. (COURTESY OF ED MONK JR.)

Throughout 1937 Monk published a "how-to-build" series, covering procedures from caulking to rigging, intended to bring cruising "to the man who loves the water but whose purse is limited." [11] These articles led to a second book, *Modern Boat Building*. "There is no better form of recreation than boating," he told his readers, "and there is something about the building of a boat that differs from the building of anything else, something that grips one's attention and stirs up latent ambitions and enthusiasm." [12] The book was filled with straightforward advice, starting with lofting, "the first step and perhaps the most difficult though not as mysterious or complicated as some would leave us to believe." [13] The V-bottom hull is faster, he explained to prospective builders; a V-bottom will plane with enough power, but the round bottom makes for a better sea boat and is easier to drive at lower speed. Expense graphs estimated that materials for the home-built, 45-foot power cruiser should cost no more than $2,935.

A considerably larger commission, the 50-foot bridge-deck cruiser *Marilyn III*, was launched in 1938, one of four sister ships built by the Lakewood Boat Company of Renton, Washington. She was bought from owner Dr. Hay by Gordon and Beverly Sullivan, and renamed *Migrator III*. In 1993 she was sold to Lew and Lindy Barrett of Seattle, who renamed her *Rita*. Like many other Puget Sound boats, she was used by the military during World War II.

More large power boats were launched in 1939, including the 50-foot *St. Elias*, and the 67-foot, Blanchard-built *Sea Rest*, which featured Maxim silencers, photo-electric piloting, and twin 165 hp Gray marine diesels.

Major Andrews' boat yard in Tacoma launched the 29-foot sloop *Sea Witch* in 1939, one of at least three boats built by Andrews from the same plan. *Sea Witch* was originally owned by Ken Metcalf, then by Dick Carlson, who sold the boat to Jack Smith of Gig Harbor in 1962. John and Jo Bailey bought *Sea Witch* in 1965; she remained in the Bailey family for the next 30 years. Jo Bailey used *Sea Witch* while researching many articles and three cruising guides, the "Gunkholing" series covering the San Juans, the Gulf Islands, and Desolation Sound. Monk designed a 43-foot ketch for the Baileys, which they called *Endeavor*, although the boat was never built. *Endeavor* was a custom version of plans used for *Southern Cross*, *Malada*, and several other ocean-going sailboats.

As money became available, Monk built a dock on the property at Port Madison, and then a dock shed for *Nan*. *Pacific Motor Boat* published his ten-dollar plans for a boatshed strong enough to withstand six feet of snow, so that owners could keep their vessels "ready to go every day of the year." [14] Monk's daughters loved their weekends at Port Madison, and the

The 16-foot "Fisherman." "My dad built this boat in 1939-40 while he had both legs in a cast for six months due to a construction accident. Built the boat crawling around on his hands and knees. Sawn oak frames, red cedar planking. Had a 15 hp outboard and went ten knots. We used it for fishing on Puget Sound." Don Sandall. [13] (COURTESY OF DON SANDALL)

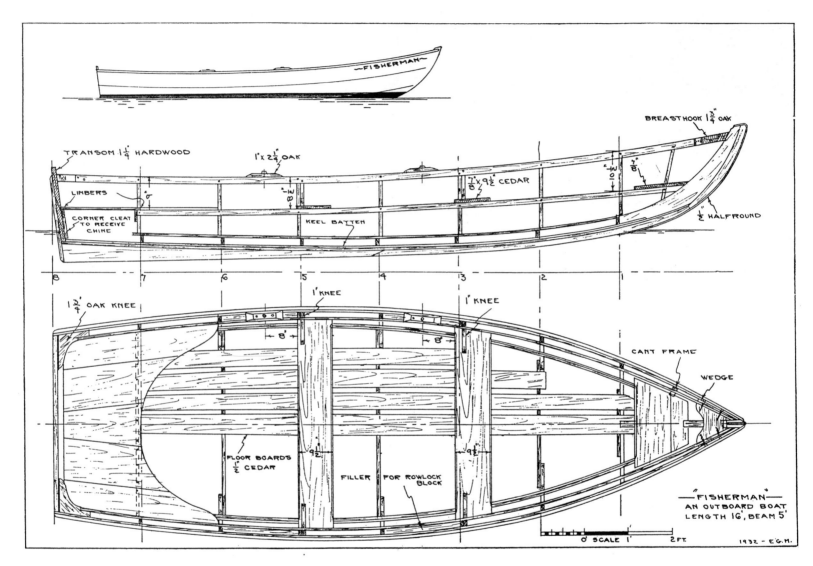

"The 'Fisherman' ... a rugged, seaworthy outboard boat suited for a long run to the fishing grounds in open water. No steam box is required, as there is no twist and the bends are not hard." Ed Monk. [14]

The Seattle Post-Intelligencer *announced the 52-foot* Swiftsure *as "The first and finest of the 1937 cruisers." Built by Doc Freeman of Fremont Boat Works as a liveaboard for Past Commodore Al Constans of Queen City Yacht Club,* Swiftsure *was originally powered with a 150 hp Superior diesel, later replaced by a 671 Gray Marine, and provided sleeping accommodation for nine. "She has been a large part of my life ever since 1946," said owner J. Ellsworth Jensen of Ketchikan, Alaska. "We just got old together."* [15] (COURTESY OF J. ELLSWORTH JENSEN)

Multi-show winner Rita *(formerly* Marilyn III, Migrator III*) much loved by owners Lew and Lindy Barrett of Seattle. Fir-planked hull over oak frames, teak cabins and interior. Twin 130 hp Nordberg engines, with a cruising speed of ten knots, top speed of 14 knots. Forward stateroom with head, steps up to the main saloon/pilothouse. Step down to the galley; large cabin aft, with dinette and settee; covered cockpit, complete with wicker furniture.* (COURTESY OF LEW AND LINDY BARRETT)

Sea Witch, *Plan No. 509, built in Tacoma, Washington, in 1939. Cedar on oak, 22 hp Palmer engine. Length 29 ft. 7 in., beam 8 ft., draft 4½ ft., displacement 12,500 lbs.* "Sea Witch *was the love of my life and we spent many happy hours aboard day sailing, weekends and four-week vacations. We raised five children aboard and all are avid sailors."* John Bailey. [16] (KEN OLLAR, 1946, COURTESY OF JOHN BAILEY)

Log of the *Nan,* August 15, 1937: "Started for our vacation 11:20. Crew consists of Keith Robison, Geoffrey Monk, family. New engine working fine 1000 rpm. Weather fine. Ate. First mate steering, bumpy, spray over bow 12:15. Chief cook and bottle washer accidentally pushed throttle. Bucking strong head wind 12:40. Captain at wheel. Possession Head — lots of boats fishing. All had a drink of Pepsicola. Fish jumping. Sea Scout boat off starboard bow. Passed Coast Guard *Ceyane.* Seaman Keith took wheel at 2:43. Crew eating apricots. First mate took wheel at 3:41. Cook and seaman shelling peas. Captain rigging up stove. Greenbanks and fields of Oak Harbor ahead. First mate relieved by Captain at wheel at 4:43. Stove works grand. Delicious odors from galley. All hands eating dinner. Very clear, Mount Baker in full view. Pretty sight. All full. AB Seaman Monk at wheel. 5:37 Ordinary Seaman Keith at wheel. Deception Pass 6:30. Crew had Pepsicola at 7:25. Fishboats, Lopez Pass ahead. Beautiful sunset. AB Seaman Monk at helm at 7:42. Getting dark. Heaved anchor at 8:06 in little bay near Decauter and Center Island. 8 hrs. 46 min. August 16: Crew up and about at 6:45. Pulled hook at 7:49. First mate steering 1000 rpm. Seaman Keith washed the windows. Cook fired pressure cooker now out in captain's domain. Fish jumping. Captain putting up towel rack. AB Seaman Monk at wheel 9:02. Seaman Keith writing letter to his girl. Crew refreshed by a Pepsicola. Keith steering, all worn out from writing letter. Passed Roche Hbr. 10:42. Fishboats coming out of harbor. Oil gauge not right. 10:58 reversed course. Oil gauge at 22. Stopped at 11:02. 11:27 started again and headed for Roche Hbr. Seaman Keith at wheel. Oil gauge at 32, stopped again 11:48 at Pearl Island. Launched large dinghy with motor and towed boat to harbor. Got there at 12:08. Engine man down to look at engine. Cracked cylinder top. Should be ready tomorrow. August 17, 18, 19: Engine being fixed. Stayed at Roche Harbor." [17] (Courtesy of Paul Helman)

(Courtesy of Paul Helman)

family often stayed over a few extra days. "It would be my sister's and my job to row him in the dinghy to, in the morning, and from, in the evening, the little steamer that traveled between Port Madison and Seattle," recalled Jo (Monk) Helman. "This was a terrible chore and we had many fights about this." [15]

Tragedy struck the family in the spring of 1939. Just as they were in the middle of planning a house, Blossom Monk suddenly and unexpectedly died. Ed Monk and his girls continued to live aboard *Nan*. After graduating from high school, Isabel went to stay with Monk's sister, Edith, in Pateros, Washington, and studied education at college, becoming a teacher. Jo enrolled in nursing at the University of Washington, walking to her classes from *Nan*'s berth at the Seattle Yacht Club. Two years later, in 1941, Ed married Anna Mary Gantz. He and his wife, who was known as Ann, bought a house in Seattle, and *Nan* was sold.

Nan, at Port Madison. (COURTESY OF PAUL HELMAN)

CHAPTER THREE

TOWBOATS AND TROLLERS

T HE ONSET OF World War II brought a surge of growth to the boatbuilding industry, with west-coast yards working nonstop to meet commissions not only from the military but also from the forestry and fishing fleets. Land was appropriated for expansion, and "maximum production" was the order of the day. Even the smaller companies like Grandy's employed 80 men, building patrol boats, launches, and tugs. Pleasure boat construction slowed, with the emphasis on craft essential to the war effort, and many private vessels were requisitioned for naval use.

Ed Monk moved his office from the Maritime Building to the Grandy Boat Company, and this is where R.F. "Tolly" Tollefson first met him, in the late 1930s. Monk designed several boats which Tollefson built for himself, then he bought a 50-foot sailboat, which he asked Monk to survey. "I was young, and I had the aspiration of sailing to the South Pacific, but I never did, the war came along." He joined the Coast Guard and worked in the Captain of the Port's office in Seattle, handling waterfront security. One of his duties was to check out boats for purchase by the War Shipping Administration, for coastal patrol. "A lot of those boats were Monk's," he recalled. [1]

With orders for lumber going out to mills all over the coast, vessels were needed to service the remote logging camps. Monk designed a 30-foot towboat for the MacDonald Logging Company of Ketchikan, Alaska. "Simple and husky," [2] it had a 90 hp gas engine, 1¾ inch by two inch bent-oak frames on ten inch centres, 1⅜ inch Alaska cedar planking, and a six inch steel channel iron running the length of the keel, extending aft to form the skeg. This vessel was joining the 36-foot towboat *Malco*, also owned by the company, drawn by Monk in 1930 when he was still associated with Geary.

New 28-Foot Plywood Towboat For Army

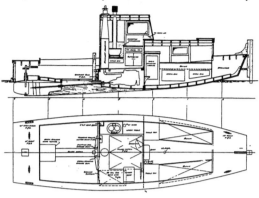

In 1943 the Army Transport Service asked for a small towboat — quick, easy, and cheap to build. Monk's solution: plywood over sawn fir frames, drawing 22 inches and powered by a Gray 4-52 gas engine, with two bunks forward and a tiny woodstove in one corner of the pilothouse. Many of these "midget river towboats" serviced the inland waterways of Alaska. [18]

"When I first talked with Ed Monk, the use of plywood seems to have been debatable, and he told me how he had arrived at his acceptable opinion of good plywood — by tacking pieces onto pilings for the alternate exposure to sea and air." Norm Collins. [19]

Contracted by the Army Transportation Corps to come up with plans for two cable-repair barges for Alaska, Monk went north to view the area where the ships would work. "This was a design problem solved only by the combination of architectural skill and the practical knowledge of the Signal Corps Officers," reported *Pacific Motor Boat*. [3] The ships were unusual in that they were triple-screw, shallow draft, with wood hulls. They were constructed by the Seattle Shipbuilding and Dry Dock Company, the first cable ships ever built and outfitted entirely with American equipment. The main engines were twin 240 hp Washington diesels; a smaller Buda diesel drove an auxiliary shaft and wheel for slow-speed operation. Completed in 1943 and 1944, *Colonel William A. Glassford* and *Basil O. Lenoir* proved very successful and remained in the repair service for many years.

The performance of the double-ender *Heron*, a new 58-foot service vessel for the Port Walter biological station of the Fish and Wildlife Service, aroused much comment in 1940. "The requirement was a double-end hull that would show some speed," explained Monk. "The orthodox double-ender is a good sea shape but to drive it at anything but a very moderate speed is almost impossible. At moderate speeds it drives very easily; but an attempt to push it beyond a given point results in a pronounced 'squat' as the hull tends to bury itself aft. This is where the long straight bottom lines of the transom stern begin to show to advantage. The objection to the transom stern for the *Heron* was that it is a poor performer in a following sea, and it has, to some eyes, a 'sawed-off' appearance. Exhaust gases have a tendency to flow into the cockpit, whereas the flow of air around a double-ender eliminates this." The *Heron*'s stern was lengthened at the waterline, and the buttocks were also extended and straightened, by superimposing a short chine or knuckle, resulting in "a clean running boat with no deep hollow in the waterline amidships." [4] Construction costs for this new type of stern were higher, but offset by an increase in speed — which Monk figured would be particularly applicable to trollers and to motor sailers. Powered by a six cylinder Murphy diesel, *Heron* cruised easily at 14 mph.

One of the few builders working on pleasure boats was Peter Lind of Bellingham, Washington, who completed the 48-foot *Nika* for George and Mary Edna Ross in 1940. The Lind Brothers yard built three more 45-foot sedan-style cruisers the following year, all with extended cabins serving the triple purpose of pilothouse, saloon, and galley. One of these was *Glorianne*, powered by a 130 hp Kermath Sea Rover. Other vessels built to similar lines were *Chilton*, at Bellingham, *Victory*, at LaConner, and *Yankee Doodle*, at the Rittner yards in Olympia. *Yankee Doodle* was originally

Profile plan for 154-foot cable-repair barge, used by U.S. Signal Corps in Alaska. (PACIFIC MOTOR BOAT, COURTESY OF PAUL HELMAN)

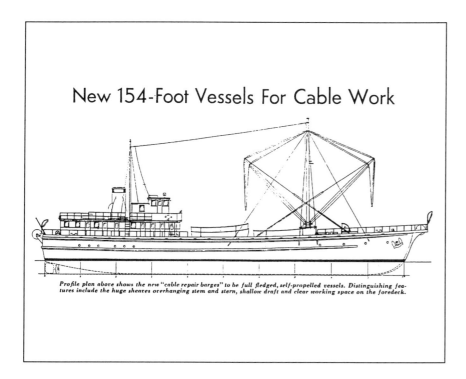

New 154-Foot Vessels For Cable Work

Profile plan above shows the new "cable repair barges" to be full fledged, self-propelled vessels. Distinguishing features include the huge sheaves overhanging stem and stern, shallow draft and clear working space on the foredeck.

Army transport boats, hulls designed by Monk, shipped by barge to Alaska. Earl Wakefield worked on these boats while employed at Puget Sound Bridge and Dredge in the early 1940s. (COURTESY OF EARL WAKEFIELD)

Nika, length 48½ ft., beam 13½ ft., draft 4 ft. 5 in. Carvel-planked cedar hull, solid mahogany topsides. Detroit 6-71 diesel engine, with a cruising speed of 8 to 12 knots. *Nika* was constructed by Lind Brothers of Bellingham in 1940, and was used for many years of cruising by owners George and Mary Edna Ross. John and Mary Ann Beveridge of Sidney, B.C., bought *Nika* in 1992, and moved aboard.

Nika was laid out with an anchor chain locker in the forepeak, and a two-berth stateroom (with locker and wash basin) immediately aft. A second cabin contained berths port and starboard. Steps led up to the main saloon, with helm station, sofas and a diesel space heater, making for a cosy living area. A step down and aft led to the rear cabin, with a convertible dinette and a head (with bathtub) on the starboard side, and a galley with a Dickinson diesel stove on the port side. The cockpit was enclosed with a hard top, and the dinghy was stored above. The washer/dryer was stored in the cockpit, which also had a built-in seat for fishing. The comfortable, canvas-enclosed fly bridge was added in 1954 and was used as the main steering station, with navigation equipment and a chart table. A swim grid was also added later, along with a transom door. "There have been no major repairs," reported owner John Beveridge, "just ongoing maintenance over the years. She sits low in the water and cuts the waves nicely without excessive roll." [20]

Nika. (COURTESY OF JOHN AND MARY ANN BEVERIDGE)

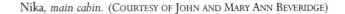

Nika, *main cabin.* (COURTESY OF JOHN AND MARY ANN BEVERIDGE)

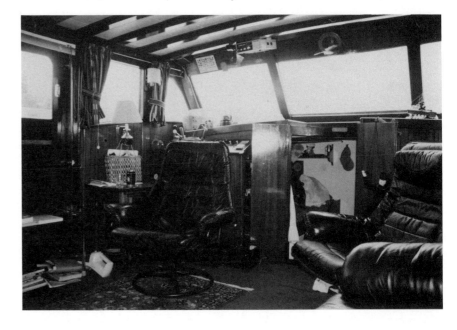

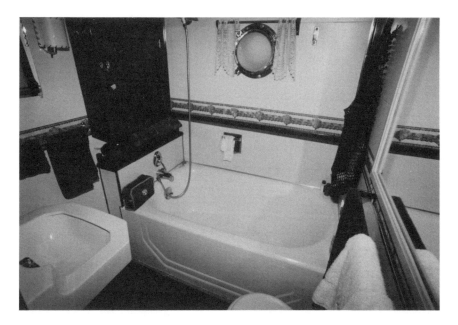

Nika*'s head.* (COURTESY OF JOHN AND MARY ANN BEVERIDGE)

Nika*'s aft cabin: galley to port, dinette to starboard.*
(COURTESY OF JOHN AND MARY ANN BEVERIDGE)

In the summer of 1956, George and Mary Edna Ross took *Nika* north up the B.C. coast, to visit Kitimat and the Gardner Canal. Mary Edna Ross shared their adventures in an article in the January 1957 issue of *SEA and Pacific Motor Boat.*

"At dawn we rose with great determination and headed the *Nika* northward. The engine purred. I was sleepy for that hour of the morning, so decided to slip back ... the water was calm and placid and I had no trouble dozing off. We proceeded up Lewis and Calm channels and then into the Yaculta Rapids.

"It was now about 7 AM and I was awakened by a sharp tugging sensation. The boat was lurching from one side to the other. I put my clothes on quickly then hopped up to the bridge beside George. We were about the middle of the Yaculta Rapids and a terrific current was running. This passage is a rather treacherous one, as the current reaches a speed at maximum of ten knots or more. It is a very picturesque and somewhat narrow channel, but when the tide is running hard the water will sweep sideways right across it and huge whirlpools will come at you from nowhere. We had hit this pass one hour before maximum flood and we were naturally having quite a time.

"Our problem was to keep the *Nika* in the center of the channel; this took some maneuvering, and George would keep telling me to watch the shoreline for fear we would be swept on to it. At one point we were at a complete standstill, with the water swirling past us. (A goat travelling along the rocky shore made better progress than we.) This was a frightening moment, especially when I saw the bow of the boat sink into one of those whirlpools. But 'luck and the Lord' travel with the *Nika,* for the bow gently rose, and she pushed on and at last sailed out of the pass. We both heaved a sigh and I hurried below to prepare our breakfast." [21]

The ex-"Glorianne" Requisitioned for War

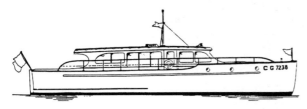

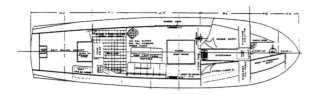

Glorianne, *requisitioned for wartime patrol as CG 7238.* (PACIFIC
MOTOR BOAT, COURTESY OF PAUL HELMAN)

equipped with a 160 hp Chrysler Majestic M-49 engine, which was replaced with an Isuzu diesel in 1986. After serving as the Olympia Yacht Club flagship for many years, *Yankee Doodle* moved to the Bremerton Yacht Club in the late 1970s when purchased by fourth owners John and Betty Metcalf of Olympia, Washington.

In 1941 the ketch *Mariner III* was launched at the Chambers and Franck yard for Peter G. Schranz. Dr. Schranz had been planning his boat through 20 years of practising dentistry in Seattle; what he envisioned was a travelling clinic, combining cruising with his work. *Mariner III* was very solidly constructed, with 1³/₈ inch red cedar planking over two inch by 2½ inch bent-oak frames on ten-inch centres, carrying 10,000 pounds of external ballast and 856 square feet of sail. A sister ship, *Sea Fever*, circumnavigated the world during a four-year voyage which began in California in 1957. Peter and Kaye Schranz were married in 1950 and they remained aboard, based out of Canoe Cove, Sidney, B.C., until his death in 1978. Second owners were Keith Richards and Anne Hatfield, friends of Claude Bigler's, who bought the boat from them in 1986 and moved aboard with his wife Diane at False Creek in Vancouver, B.C. "When the surveyor came to inspect *Mariner III*, he marveled at her condition. She was dry as a bone, no leaks, no dry rot. Her wood — red cedar on oak — was from mature trees painted with red lead during assembly, which is why the boat is so well preserved." [5]

The Grandy Boat Company was commissioned by Adolf Schmidt to build his 62-foot *Winifred III*, described in local newspapers as one of the finest recent additions to the Puget Sound pleasure craft fleet. The 56-foot fir keel was supplied by the Pacific National Lumber Company of Tacoma. The engine compartment was sound-proofed, and exhaust from the 150 hp Buda 909 diesel was carried by a heavy rubber pipe through a water-filled tank at the stern of the engine room. "Cooled and silenced," [6] the exhaust vapours were vented upwards in a hollow, aluminum mast. With hot-water heating and a drying compartment in the bathroom, *Winifred III* set new standards for refinement. In addition to the Buda diesel, a Chrysler Ace auxiliary motor was mounted under the cockpit, recommended by Monk for driving the boat at trolling speed.

Now that *Nan* was sold, Monk needed another boat for his own use, and in 1940 he arranged for the Grandy yard to build his 24-foot *Port Madison Gal*. With a planing hull and a direct drive 75 hp Chrysler Ace, she ran at 18 mph. The cabin sides were built of marine plywood, an opportunity for Monk to personally test this new product, although the common plywood used on the interior of *Nan* had stood up well.

Mariner III, *Plan No. 417, length 42 ft., beam 13 ½ ft., draft 6 ft. "This boat is designed to be handled by one person in conditions up to thirty knots, without reef. Its worm gear makes steering very easy, with no pressure on the wheel, which is tiring.* Mariner *has been cruised between Seattle, Alaska, and Hawaii numerous times ... and has been a liveaboard for its entire life. There have been no major repairs or renovations, mainly diligent upkeep by all owners. The strength of* Mariner's *style and design is a seaworthiness — it is truly a beautiful liveaboard with lots of storage for long voyages."* Claude Bigler. [22] (COURTESY OF ED MONK JR.)

above: On a reef in Alaska. **Mariner III** *also grounded on a beach in Hawaii, surviving both incidents without damage.* (COURTESY OF CLAUDE BIGLER)

above and left: **Mariner III,** *with the Red Cross emblem displayed above deck, and a collapsible dentist chair down below. Dr. Peter Schranz and his wife Kaye provided dental and medical service to fishermen and families during 30 years of cruising along the B.C. and Alaska coast.* (COURTESY OF CLAUDE BIGLER)

The war was placing a burden on all the country's transportation resources, particularly the forestry and fishing fleets, challenging naval architects and builders to come up with more efficient designs. The traditional troller, carrying five tons of ice with a slow-turning motor, was limited to seven or eight knots. A faster boat meant less time running to the fishing banks, and in 1940 Monk published plans for a troller capable of 12 knots, with twin engines driving a single shaft through a reduction gear. "The V-bottom shape was chosen because with the lighter boat some advantages in this shape are apparent. Although not light enough to plane, the chine line aft combines with the pointed stern to form a flat run. Little, if any, ballast is contemplated with this type of hull." [7]

The lines for the troller were developed with the help of Seattle propeller expert Don Thomas, using scale models to try out the different hull shapes. Monk was one of the first designers to test his theories by building models; with no testing tanks available in the northwest, he towed his models along the shore of Lake Union, near the Grandy yard. His test results were used by other naval architects, and were published in the reference book *Hydrodynamics in Ship Design* by William Saunders, in 1957.

The troller was followed by a design for a 32-foot seiner which was an immediate success: Grandy built three for the San Juan Fishing and Packing Company, and three more for the Washington Fish and Oyster Company, all powered by Chrysler Ace gas engines. Three heavy-duty 48-foot trollers were built to a new design later in 1941, with dry exhaust, Chrysler Crown engines and a cruising speed of 11 knots. The trollers had fir timbers and decking, with a plywood pilothouse; the stern, similar to *Heron*, featured a short chine for added speed and roominess.

Seattle fisherman William Anderson requested plans for a combination-type 60-footer, which was built by Andy Edwards Shipyard in Edmonds, Washington, in 1944. The full, rounded hull and buoyant stern of the combination boat gave added versatility: a seiner-type dragger could be converted to fish for tuna, shark, or halibut. Or, with a turntable mounted on the stern, the vessel could be used for purse seining for salmon. Anderson's boat was equipped with an 85 hp Atlas diesel and accommodation for eight, with six berths in the forecastle.

Of all the types of fishing, otter trawling — or "dragging" — in offshore waters placed the most rigorous demands on the vessels, the crew, and the gear. A net and heavy gear — the otter boards — are scraped along the ocean floor, "with the vessel functioning for all the world like a tug for hours on end." [8] Two new 60-foot "drag" boats were completed for veteran trawl fishermen, from a similar design to the one commissioned by

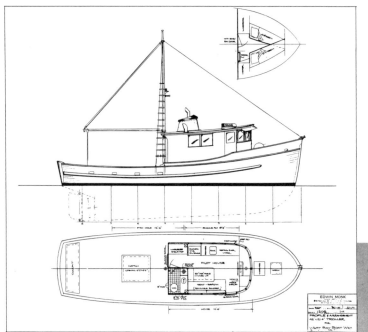

left: Plan No. 1205 with transom stern. Monk drew several versions of this traditional-hulled troller, and hundreds were built throughout the northwest. (COURTESY OF ED MONK JR.)

below: Aurora, 42-foot troller from Plan No. 1205. (COURTESY OF ED MONK JR.)

Anderson, with a double break in the sheer line and the pilothouse situated well toward the bow, protected by the raised foredeck. First was *Zarembo III*, for Howard Brondson, at the Marine View Boat Building yard in Tacoma. *Tralee* for William White was launched in May at the Astoria Marine Construction Company in 1941.

Grandy built the 40-foot *Springbok II* in 1941, a forerunner of the trademark "troller-type cruiser" Monk became renowned for after the war. Seaworthy but comfortably laid out, the double-ended *Springbok II* was commissioned by Gordon Wilson for use in the Coast Guard Reserve at Port Angeles, where Lieutenant Wilson was stationed as captain of the port. *Springbok II* was powered by a Chrysler Royal and had a cruising range of 650 miles at 8½ knots. The plans were published in *Pacific Motor Boat*, creating a stir of interest not only among future yacht owners but also from the Royal Canadian Air Force in Ottawa, resulting in an order in 1944 for six blueprints. "The RCAF require some boats for patrolling practice bombing ranges, which are located on the East Coast, and their location is such that the crew must remain at sea for periods of four to five days at a time. Your design ... appears to be very suitable to meet our requirements." [9]

When the war ended, many of the smaller yards returned to building fishing boats. Clark Brothers, at Brentwood Bay on southern Vancouver Island, employed a steady crew of seven and launched four trollers in quick succession: the 40-foot *Zenith*, and three 42-footers, *Sultan*, *Laparose* and *Arabella II*. Later they built two 38-footers, *Kevalla* and *Princess Pat*.

Alex North, who had a yard at Finn Bay near Lund on the B.C. Sunshine Coast, built six 41-foot trollers between 1946 and 1949: *Galley Bay*, *Norlite*, *Lor-Dell II*, *Wanderer No. 2*, *Adolfina*, and *Finn Bay*. *Galley Bay*, owned by Ed Hansen, was outfitted with one of the "new" 110 hp Chrysler Crown engines and taken north to fish for tuna and salmon off the Queen Charlotte Islands. Other than replacing the gas engine with a Gardner 6LW diesel in 1960, Ed Hansen maintained his boat in its original condition, fishing every year for more than four decades.

Bill Osborne, working at a yard beside Alberni Engineering at Port Alberni, B.C., completed *Solander Isle* for Don Bostrum over the winter of 1946. "I must have built at least 16 boats designed by Mr. Monk," he recalled. "The first one — for Jack Kampe of Ucluelet — a 37-foot deep sea troller, in 1945." This was followed by a 36-foot day troller, then the 40-foot *Solander Isle*. Most of the boats had four or six cylinder Chrysler gas engines. "Diesels at that time, at trolling speed, would foul up so gas engines were prevalent." He later built two Monk-designed power

Henry Clark founded Clark Brothers Boat Works in 1938, with his brother Stan. Like many of his profession, Henry, surrounded by boats, did not own one himself after his early 20s. When he retired, Henry recorded his life's work in his photograph albums, with the same care and attention received by every vessel that left the Clark Brothers shop.

"We started out with Thornton Grenfell; we grew up together and worked together. We came over to Brentwood in 1938, and when the war came along, we went to join the navy. They wouldn't accept us, only as seamen, and we said you take us as petty officers or come and get us. I kept the shop open — we built lifeboats for the government, 200 or so. Right after the war, the west-coast tuna troller came in, designed by Monk. The first one we built was for Joe Halstrom, a 40-footer. Of course, being boatbuilders, we have our own ideas, and we asked Monk if we could add two feet. He agreed, and we added the two feet; with the same engine, the boat went faster and carried a bigger load. These boats had Chrysler Crowns, and some went to diesel later. All fir planking, very heavily built. Sometimes we would have as many as four boats going at a time on the floor.

"Some other Monk jobs went to Victoria or Vancouver; some of them put bait tanks on deck, and on the trials they tipped over. The fishermen came to us, and some of them wanted changes — fishermen are famous for that — and we told them 'Go get it drawn up by Monk.' We thought highly of Ed Monk, and he came up now and again, and he thought highly of us.

"Wooden boatbuilding is a thing of the past. There are very few people who call themselves boatbuilders who can just take a set of offsets and build a boat. People ask, where did you and your brother learn the trade? I say, where did the first boatbuilder learn his trade? You have a feel for boats, you go by trial and error, and after a while, you've got it. It's a gift." [23]

above: Seiner Tongareva. (RAY KRANTZ, COURTESY OF FRED BAILEY)

left: Seiners Shelikof *and* Tongareva, *built by Grandy in the early 1940s.* (RAY KRANTZ, COURTESY OF FRED BAILEY)

Tuna troller Arabella II, built by Clark Brothers for George Westinghouse. Powered by a 60 hp 36A Fairbanks-Morse and an auxiliary 5 hp Onan diesel. With a Bendix echo sounder, radio-phone, direction finder, hydraulic winch and gurdies, Wagner Pilot and hydraulic steering, Arabella II was well equipped for its time. (COURTESY OF HENRY CLARK)

left: Solander Isle, *making a final run in a gale off Estevan Point, on the west coast of Vancouver Island.* "I have fished for 14 years on the west coast and central coast," *said skipper Lee Morris, in 1997,* "and have always known the boat to be way tougher than I am." [24] (COURTESY OF LEE MORRIS)

below: Solander Isle, *built for Don Bostrum in 1946.* (COURTESY OF LEE MORRIS)

cruisers: *Hotei* for Mr. Douglas, and the other for his brother Robert, of Osborne Propellers, in North Vancouver. "Mr. Monk was a real gentleman, treated me very well. Dropped around from time to time." [10]

Don Bostrum retired to his home overlooking Esquimalt harbour, B.C., where for many years he kept his boats. His father had come out to Seattle from Sweden, then moved to Kyuquot on the northwest coast of Vancouver Island, where Don grew up and raised a family of his own. He named his boat after Solander Island off Cape Cook, "a beautiful rock when it's not blowing, which is hardly ever," and fished from Washington to the Queen Charlotte Islands. "It was a good boat, the *Solander Isle*. Big rudder, excellent handling, but it did roll. We didn't have a depthsounder at first; we got one soon after, and then radar. Those early boats were basic; we had an anchor winch but no hydraulics in those days." [11]

Don Bostrum sold the boat to Dave Slaco in 1971, when he had a larger one built. Lee Morris of Saltspring Island, B.C., bought *Solander Isle* in 1983 and maintained her lovely condition, keeping her topsides freshly painted and her cap rails varnished. The gas engine had been exchanged for a 453 GM Detroit diesel, giving a cruising speed of seven to 7½ knots. "Her high bow and bulwarks make her a fairly dry boat," said Lee Morris. "Smallish cabin — in the 1940s fishboats were designed to pack fish, not to be comfy! Don told me that he packed 16,000 pounds of halibut in the hold, which is now fibreglass. She has a full horseshoe stern end with a very flat counter, enabling it to lift easily in a following sea. Large batwings have been added at some point to the mid keel. Heavily built throughout ... the wheelhouse is bolted from roof to hull every 16 inches with six foot by ½ inch bolts, and the planking below the waterline is mostly stem to stern with no butts. She was certainly designed to weather anything that she would encounter." [12]

One of several tugboat commissions received by Monk after the war, the 40-foot *Hookline No. 3* was drawn for the Alaska Packers Association and subsequently built by Outer Harbor Marine Ways, Tacoma, Washington, in 1946. *Hookline No. 3* was later owned by several Puget Sound lumber mills, used for towing log booms. In 1983, Vern and Shirley Sampson of Sointula, B.C., purchased the tug for charter work. The tug's plans had included drawings for a tunnel stern, with only 32 inches of draft. "She was built with the more conventional stern," reported Vern Sampson, "which I think has contributed to her longevity. The tunnel stern would be difficult to recaulk or repair over the years." [13]

The 38-foot troller *Bonnie Belle*, constructed from plans drawn in 1946, was launched in 1950 at Ocean Falls, B.C. *Bonnie Belle* was bought by John

When asked if he had any particular memories of fishing off the rugged northwest corner of Vancouver Island, Don Bostrum laughed. "No, it was just common, ordinary misery." He did recall one incident, though, at the treacherous Nitinat Bar.

"We went into Nitinat; we'd been there lots of times, packing fish. We were getting ready to leave this one time, and the Indian says, wait till I wave. I thought it was the wrong time, but he waved and I went. He had meant for us not to go, but I didn't know, all I could see was him standing on the beach there, waving ....

"We met some huge big breakers, and the boat started going around .... Well, there's always three big waves, then seven small ones, and you're supposed to go when the big waves are just finished and then you've got lots of time to get out of there. Well, this huge wave came, and I thought it was going to come right through the window. But the bow just split the waves, and the boat started going backwards, and the kettle jumped right off the stove. My partner was standing by the stove, and the kettle hit him in the chest, it took such a jump. By this time the boat was pushed backwards and sideways, a little bit at a time. A bunch of the penboards floated off and the boat was filled with water right up to the door. The whole stern went under the water. Fortunately, everything was tight. The boat was heavy, full of dog salmon — we got $24,000 for that load.

"By the time the third wave was there, it was right broadside. If there had been a fourth one, I don't know what would have happened. Anyways, it got calm and away we went. I was going full speed, and I don't know whether the keel was on the bottom or what. So we were glad to get out of there.

"When we came back in, the next trip, the Indians came down alongside the log booms where we used to tie, where the old cannery was. 'We thought you were goners,' they said. They'd picked up some of our ...

penboards off the beach. It didn't hurt the boat any. I thought for sure it was going to take the windows out, quite a few boats have lost their windows at Nitinat. Luckily our boat had lots of flare in the bow. They lost a whole cannery crew there one time, when the canning season was over. I don't know how many people were on this boat, but they went out and got in one of those breakers, and they were all lost. The bar is shallow." [25]

above and below: Hookline No. 3. (COURTESY OF VERN SAMPSON)

Hookline No. 3, length 40 ft., beam 12½ ft., draft 5 ft. 1⅜ inch fir planking, sheathed in gumwood, on oak frames. 165 hp Gray Marine 6-71 GM diesel; twin disc — manual clutch with 2:1 reduction. 26 inch by 26 inch four-blade Michigan propeller, with 2¼ inch shaft. Cast bronze rudder and skeg. Built in 1946, owned since 1983 by Vern and Shirley Sampson of Sointula, B.C., who have chartered the boat and their services to the Canadian Department of Fisheries and Oceans. "She is a familiar sight to the salmon fishing fleet in the Rivers Inlet, Bella Bella area. We work with both the commercial and the sports fish sectors, gathering catch statistics and other Fisheries management tasks. In the early fall you will often find the *Hookline No. 3* anchored off the estuaries of rivers with names like Quartcha, Nekite, Takush, while the owner is hiking up the river counting returning salmon stocks and trying not to disturb the grizzlies!

"I imagine that Mr. Monk could not have envisioned the array of electronics that now fill the wheelhouse ... radar, radio-telephone, scanners, autotel with fax machine and even a computer. And yes, she still has a towpost. Even though *Hookline No. 3* is more or less retired from serious towboat work, we used her to tow our floathouse around Rivers Inlet a few years ago." Vern Sampson. [26]

MT-281 *36-foot tunnel type towboat built in 1943 by the Grandy Boat Company for the U.S War Department.* (Ray Krantz, courtesy of Fred Bailey)

Bonnie Belle, *38-foot troller owned since 1953 by John Parkyn, Campbell River, B.C. Andy Carrie was the "builder and driving force behind her creation," said John Parkyn. "Although she was designed and built as a west-coast troller, she was never rigged out and fished commercially. She has done a number of jobs over the years, a little towing and freighting, commercial charters of various kinds, and in more recent years mostly sports fishing trips. The plans showed a Mack diesel but she was launched with a Chrysler Crown gas engine and 4:1 gear, which is still in service after several rebuilds and block replacements over the years. There have been no structural changes, which I suppose is a little unusual for a wooden vessel of her age." [27] (COURTESY OF JOHN PARKYN)*

Parkyn of Campbell River, B.C., in 1953 and was used for skippered charters out of Campbell River, an area famous for attracting sport fishermen from around the world. *Bonnie Belle*'s nine-foot tender was later replaced by an updated version of Monk's original design. "The dinghy that came with the boat when I bought her had got to be in pretty rough shape after 20 years of hard use," John Parkyn explained. "So I wrote to Ed Monk and told him what a good model it had been and did he still have the plans. He very kindly sent them to me 'no charge' and with the suggestion that we raise the sheer line a couple of inches. A friend of mine on Quadra Island subsequently built it for me and made a beautiful job. We used traditional copper roves on the gunwales and copper, bronze, or stainless fastenings throughout, with gumwood protective runners on the bottom and along the chine, and she's holding up very well, ³/₈ inch red cedar on yellow cedar frames." [14]

Monk's own experience on the water, along with his overriding concern for safety, gave him an appreciation for the conditions endured by west-coast fishermen. When the fishing season opens, his trollers and seiners head out from their home ports, still working after more than 50 years.

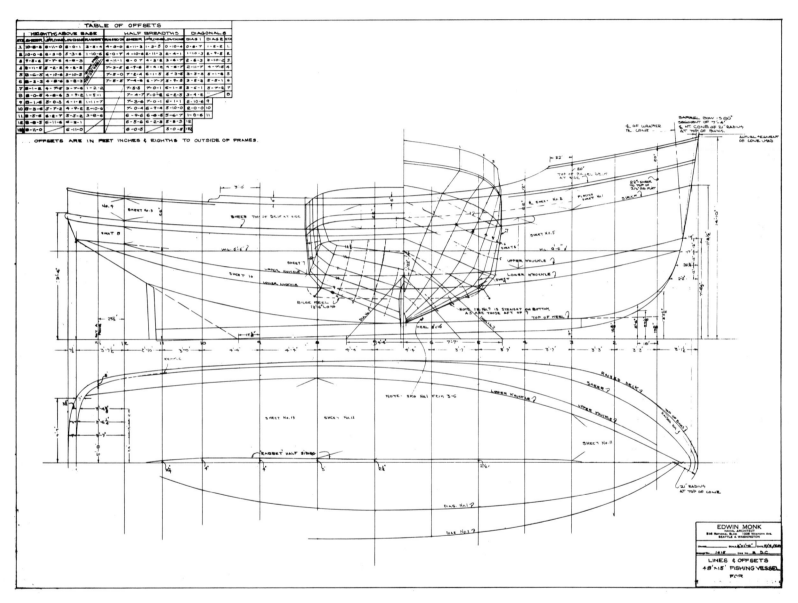

*Plan No. 1415, lines and offsets of fishing vessel, length 48 ft.,
beam 15 ft. (COURTESY OF ED MONK JR.)*

Troller ready for launching at Clark Brothers Boat Works, Brentwood Bay, B.C., 1945. (HERBERT CLARK, COURTESY OF HENRY CLARK)

CHAPTER FOUR

THE POST-WAR BOOM

"THE NEXT BIG fleet to be launched into the Pacific will be an armada of pleasure craft, mostly conservative in design, many already planned ahead," predicted Monk in 1944. Contracts for fishing boats were replacing military projects, but, with the passing of this commercial peak, it would be pleasure boats that sustained the west-coast yards. A national survey placed the recreational boating industry far ahead of cars, new houses, or even household appliances in the percentage of growth from 1940 to 1946, and there were signs that the Pacific coast would be well ahead of the country's average. The Seattle area had 23,000 registered boats in 1941, second only to New York. "Looking ahead, it's easy, too, to find on every hand the evidence of new thousands of potential boat owners. One group is the seven or eight thousand non-boat-owners now taking an active part in Coast Guard Auxiliary doings; another is the huge total of newly boat-minded men created by the wide-scale boat operations in the Pacific theatre of war." [1]

Most appealing to these potential boaters were the stock, sedan-style designs around 30 feet in length, pioneered during the 1920s by companies like Blanchard, Grandy, and Lake Union Construction and Dry Dock Company. Through their wartime experience of meeting government contracts, builders had discovered the savings in large-scale production and the use of plywood and resin glues. Bonded laminates, easily adapted to the skills of backyard boaters, proved successful on a series of 30-foot shallow-draft tenders Monk designed for an Alaska packing company. Planking on the tenders, described as "unusual," [2] consisted of an inner ¼ inch layer of plywood diagonal strips, and an outer ¾ inch layer of yellow cedar planks laid lengthwise. The layers were bonded with resin glue and fastened with screws onto the frames.

left: The Grandy yard. (RAY KRANTZ, COURTESY OF FRED BAILEY)

below: Grandy's KLATAWA, *a fine example of the many pleasure boats built in the Pacific Northwest right after World War II.* (RAY KRANTZ, COURTESY OF FRED BAILEY)

The 75-foot Chula Mia, *commissioned in 1945 by businessman C. W. Myers of Portland, Oregon, was considered by many to be one of the most beautiful boats that Monk ever designed.* (LAWRENCE BARBER, COURTESY OF FRED BAILEY)

Fred Bailey, son of Grandy partner Henry Bailey, worked at the yard from 1953 to 1965. "I remember my father showing me around the company in the 1940s, and seeing Mr. Monk's blueprints. I was then able to see the boats being built by the most talented shipwrights in the Pacific Northwest. I especially remember the *Chula Mia*, and *Sea Swallow*." [28]

"When I first started working on boats, going to school [1937], the first boats we built, the structural bulkheads were double diagonal, tongue in groove fir or mahogany. Then came the advent of plywood. Plywood was already in use when I went to school but they didn't trust it in the boatbuilding business, yet. Pretty soon the plywood was getting better and better, and they started using it for the bulkheads. Pretty soon they were using it for the cabinsides, and pretty soon they were using it for the deck, and then they were building the whole boat out of plywood, in the early 1940s. Then came the fibreglass boat — I was teaching at Edison Technical School one day in the 1950s and a guy came out to the shop with a 14-foot boat on a trailer. It was the most godawful-looking thing as far as the workmanship .... The chicken wire mandril was still in it, part of the structure, like a mould, only with the fibreglass mat on the inside and the outside. It was kind of a green-coloured resin after it cured; you could look right through it. Now there's very little wood on a boat, except for the joiner work." Earl Wakefield, founder of the Admiral Boat Company. [29]

Even newer materials — flexible glass, synthetic varnish, and moulded plastics — offered advantages that seemed almost too good to be true. Advancements in reduction gear and diesel engines would benefit larger boats, "for the man of means," while for smaller vessels gas remained the practical choice. The war had not brought any significant improvements in hull design, noted Monk. "It still takes just as much horsepower to push so many tons on a given waterline as it ever did." The biggest attraction of the larger cruisers would be their equipment: fingertip controls, ship-to-shore radio-telephone, depth finder, electric toilet, lightweight plastic or plywood dinghy, engine-compartment blower, sound insulation, fresh-water cooling, and an automatic fire-extinguishing system. For smaller boats, there would only be minor changes, and as for sailboats, their owners were "a conservative lot." [3]

The Coast Guard reported that there were 90,000 documented boats on the Pacific coast in 1946, an increase since the last survey in 1938 of no less than 168%. "Backlogs on the books of boatbuilders and dealers that extend well into 1947 attest to the fact that many, many more boats could be built and sold, the demand is so great and the public today so boat-minded." [4] The Sparkman & Stephens design firm echoed that finding on the east coast, while in Seattle, naval architects H. C. Hanson and William Garden were kept busy with new commissions. Lorne Garden, William's brother, formed a partnership with Monk which continued through the early 1950s. Monk's son, Ed Jr., remembered visiting the office as a child and asking Lorne Garden for sketches of his favourite cartoons. "Many of the drawings in our files have Lorne's signature on them," he added, "and they are definitely his. He was a very good stylist, just like his brother Bill." [5]

Some of the most enthusiastic buyers were the car dealers: Lyman Thomas, head of the Seattle Packard Company, contracted Blanchard Boat Company to build his 50-foot cruiser. "The new boat will be modernistic in every respect with its streamlined hull, barrel bow, rounded transom stern and its new Wilcox-Crittenden marine-type windows that open like portlights. Its power plant will be a pair of Packard super-eight marine gas engines ... giving the boat a top speed of close to 20 knots." [6] For added room, the engines were placed under hinged hatches in the cockpit; the galley and dinette were on the same level as the pilothouse, an arrangement that had worked well in recent designs.

Margo, a 42-foot power cruiser, was launched from the Grandy yard in 1946, with a carvel-planked Alaska cedar hull. *Margo* was followed by the 40-foot *Donna Ray*, later named *Thunderbird*, and the 40-foot *Ailsa Craig*, in 1949.

Also in 1946, the 36-foot double-ender *Holiday* was built at the Chambers boat yard on Lake Union, by Jim Chambers, Vic Franck, and Earl Wakefield. A robust little ship, *Holiday* carried two tons of lead ballast and had a fir keel, oak ribs, Port Orford cedar planking, and canvas-covered plywood decks. The original engine was a Chrysler Crown, which was replaced with a six cylinder Ford diesel, giving a cruising speed of eight knots. The head and berths were situated forward, with the wheelhouse above the engine room amidships, and the dinette and galley aft. Skipper Rex Bartlett and his wife Verda took *Holiday* twice to Alaska, twice to the Queen Charlotte Islands, and three times around Vancouver Island. In 1985, the Bartletts passed *Holiday* on to their grandson, Dan Bartlett, of Marysville, Washington. Dan had grown up on the boat, helping his grandparents maintain it, and looked forward to years of cruising with his own family.

An old friend of Rex and Verda Bartlett's, a sea captain, gave them some good advice. "A spirit of adventure is what it takes," he said, "and them as haven't got it better stay away from boats." Heading home in *Holiday* from Prince Rupert one summer in the early 1950s, Rex and Verda reached Browning Entrance near Banks Island at nightfall, but were unable to locate the marker light. "When at last we found it, then we couldn't tell from our chart just where the channel lay. Again we studied our chart and read its direful warning: Numerous drying rocks. The skipper was grim. 'Guess there's nothing left to do,' he said, 'but head out to sea till morning.'

"While contemplating this gloomy prospect, suddenly we saw it. A bright light gleaming out from the side of a tall building beyond which looked to be the faint outline of fishboats. Our spirits took a joyful leap. Should we take a chance and go in? Perhaps if we went very slowly and kept well over toward the light. The skipper reduced the engine to its lowest speed, lined up the lights, and proceeded to move in slowly and very cautiously. When we reached a point just beyond the tall building he shut off the motor. As the anchor winch began its slow, steady grind, the ship's clock responded with its clear ringing call of eight bells. Midnight.

"We awoke late the next morning to find the bay full of boats so we moved in closer and tied up at the float. The fishermen gave us a hearty welcome, and when we told them that we had come in during the night, they at first couldn't believe it. No one, they said, except fishermen, fish buyers, freight boats, and such ever came in there under any circumstances, and they were so familiar with the place that no channel markings were necessary. Besides — and this set us back on our heels with a thump

Holiday carried owners Rex and Verda Bartlett all over the Pacific Northwest. In the days before Loran, GPS and radar, navigating presented some challenges. In the late 1950s, they set off on their third circumnavigation of Vancouver Island. At Bull Harbour, on the north tip of the island, they waited and waited for the right conditions to round Cape Scott. "When the weather report was finally favorable, we headed out to sea. As we moved out into Queen Charlotte Sound the sea grew rougher, but straightened out after we'd passed the light and turned left toward Cape Scott. It would take us about three hours to get to Cape Scott and for the first two hours of the trip the sea was calm and the predicted fog patches nothing to worry about. Then the fog got thicker until the shoreline was invisible.

" 'Here's where our depth finder starts paying its way,' said the skipper. 'When we run out three hours time we'll know we're there. Then all we've got to do is match up the markings on our depth finder with those on our chart and go on around. Can't miss.'

"For some time we continued our regular speed, then Rex slowed. 'The way I figure it,' he said, 'this is it. Here we go.' Slowly he made the turn, one eye on the depth finder, the other on the chart.

"For another half hour we cruised slowly along, still in dense fog. Then it started to lift and back to our left we could see the very tip of Cape Scott. By 10:30 we were opposite Sea Otter Cove and dropped anchor." [30]

above: Holiday, *one of the first of the "troller-cruisers."* (COURTESY OF EARL WAKEFIELD)

right: Holiday *in the 1990s, owned by the Bartlett family since 1946.* (COURTESY OF DAN BARTLETT)

— the bright light on the side of the building was not supposed to be left on all night. Last night someone had just forgotten to turn it off.

" 'You folks were just lucky,' the fishermen told us. And as we looked out at the many jagged rocks that now at low tide were clearly visible, we heartily agreed." [7]

The next two boats Monk designed for himself were bridge-deck cruisers. The 40-foot *Western Maid I*, outfitted with a single 143 hp Chrysler Royal engine, was built by Bud Forder of Bothell, Washington, in 1946. The 42-foot *Western Maid II*, built at the Grandy yard in 1947, had twin 95 hp Chrysler Crown engines and was capable of 20 knots. "In the years right after the war we gradually tumbled to the fact that boats didn't have to be so heavy," Monk said. [8] Among his solutions to keep a light-weight hull strong were "floating ribs" [9] in the forward section — strips of oak which lay beside the regular ribs, fastened to each plank between the chine and keel.

Many yards were putting out the popular 30-footers, one of which, by the Admiral Boat Company, attracted the interest of Vic Griffin in 1946. Earl Wakefield, founder of the company, was the force behind what eventually became Admiral Marine Works in Port Angeles, one of North America's principal yacht builders. The sumptuous 161-foot *Evviva*, a William Garden design launched from Admiral Marine in the mid-1990s, was at that time the second-largest GRP vessel ever constructed in the U.S. Like many Puget Sound boatbuilders, Earl Wakefield learned his trade at Edison Technical School in Seattle, where he later worked as an instructor, from 1950 to 1976. "The first time I went into business with anyone was about 1943, Chambers Boat Company," he recalled. "Jim Chambers, his son, and myself — we leased the boatbuilding school from Edison Technical School because it was just standing empty; they didn't have any students because everyone had gone off to fight the war. You couldn't build pleasure boats during the war — you couldn't get the materials. You could build fish boats …. we built the *Minker* and the *Rebel*, sister ships, at Chambers. We also built a 46-foot seiner, the *Melody*. We built three 39-footers right at the end of the war — bridge-deck, with a mahogany house — they cost $18,000, complete, with Chrysler Royal straight eight engines.

"Ed Monk's plans were very good to build, and he was very easy to deal with. If you could see some advantage in changing something, he would always listen to you. I started building his boats when I was a student, working on the *Kiletan*, Hugh Garrett's boat, and we did many more. Around 1947 we phased out Chambers Boat Company because the school came back in, and that's when I started Admiral Boat Company." [10]

Hi-Seas, owned from 1947 to 1997 by Vic Griffin, who was well known around Vancouver Island from his years as an oil-company representative.

"My first association with Ed Monk goes back to 1946, when I decided to build a boat. I went down to see Ed in Seattle, as we had corresponded for a little while about what I wanted. It was the first boat show that Seattle had, in a big marquee opposite Bryant's Marina on a vacant lot. I had gone to see Ed at his office, and he said, 'I think you better go down to the boat show, and take a look at the boat in there by Admiral Boat Company, and then come back and tell me how that would suit you.' So I went to the show and walked into the tent, and there it was. I didn't even look at another boat. I said to my wife, 'There's the boat.' We went aboard and talked to a fellow by the name of Earl Wakefield, the owner of Admiral Boat Company. I explained what I was doing there, and Earl shut the gate, and we sat down and talked about the boat. We were quite happy with the design and layout, so I went back and told Ed Monk, 'I think those plans will be okay.' 'I thought so, too,' he said.

"I bought the plans and got everything ready to build the boat. Then I went down to the States on a holiday, and came by the Admiral Boat Company and went in to see Earl. 'Have you started the boat yet?' he asked. I said, 'No, I want the lumber list in front of me, if I can get it. I brought you a bottle of good Scotch whisky.' We sat on a pile of lumber and had a drink, and he called his foreman over and sent him into the office to make out a list. Then he said, 'But you know you're not going to build that boat.' 'What do you mean?' I asked. 'I've had the plans revised,' he said, 'adding two feet. So I'll phone Ed and have him send you the new plans.'

"In the process of building the boat I was going back and forth to Seattle, and every time I went down I'd visit Ed, and we became good friends. He seemed very happy doing what he was doing. My …

Hi-Seas, coming through the Pender Islands. (COURTESY OF VIC GRIFFIN)

plans cost $45, and in 1947 that was a lot of money, but he had a reputation for being very good and very fair. His office was modest, didn't have all the elaborate things that offices have now. If the phone rang, he picked it up.

"In those days all you had in any boat was an oil burner stove, an ice box, and we had inside controls, sleeping accommodation in the bow for two, a head, and a dinette which folded down. We had a pump and 40 gallons of fresh water, 90 gallons of fuel. The electric lights ran off the battery. We just had generators on the engines, not alternators where you can pull the batteries back up fast. Batteries were a problem — you didn't sit around all night with the lights on. There was no winch; we had a Northill anchor with manila rope." [31]

Wendy A in 1951, alongside Edison Technical School, on Lake Union in Seattle, Washington, where the troller was built.
(COURTESY OF EARL WAKEFIELD)

above: Second Seattle Boat Show, 1947, held at the Washington National Guard Armory. (COURTESY OF EARL WAKEFIELD)

right: The Admiral Boat Company had three 28-foot sedan cruisers ready for the first Seattle Boat Show, and sold them all. "This was an exciting time for us," recalled Earl Wakefield and his wife, Dora. By the time the next show came around, they were building 30-footers, then 32-footers, moving the moulds a little farther apart, keeping the boats "nice and fair." (32) (COURTESY OF EARL WAKEFIELD)

right: Laying the teak deck on **Lady Jean**. (COURTESY OF EARL WAKEFIELD)

below: The 1947 launching of the 40-foot bridge-deck cruiser Keewaydin, *from the Admiral Boat Company on the Duwamish River, Seattle.* Keewaydin, *for Dr. C. Stone, was followed by the 42-foot, black-hulled* Lady Jean. (COURTESY OF EARL WAKEFIELD)

Earl Wakefield started off whittling models of boats and airplanes as a teenager, an interest which led him to a job with Ed Monk, building towing models of hulls Monk was designing for the navy. Not long after finishing boatbuilding school in 1939, Earl went to work at the Seattle-Tacoma Shipyard, which had started up on Harbor Island, in Elliot Bay, Seattle, with an order for ten destroyers. "So they sent me over with the original crew to help them get going, because they were looking all over the country for workers, scraping the bottom of the barrel for talent, and most of the people needed to be trained. I worked on the destroyers for a year or so, and then I worked on the big ships as a shipwright. Mostly I was on lines, because I had the experience from going to school." After a stint at Puget Sound Bridge and Dredge, also on Harbor Island, Earl got a call from Sea Bell Shipbuilding Company, which was building 230-foot ocean-going barges, *Douglas Fir I, II, III,* and *IV.* "What's the pay?" he asked. "Two fish," replied the superintendent. "Two dollars an hour." Earl was put in charge of lofting and planking, and when he saw the "acres of bottom" on his first barge, he decided to go to Jim Chambers, his boatbuilding instructor at Edison, for some advice. "The first garboard was 8½ inches by 15 inches, the second garboard was 6½ inches by 14 inches, and the bottom planking was four inches by 12 inches ... and the heaviest planking I had ever put on a boat was about an inch and an eighth. 'Well, Earl,' said Jim Chambers, 'it's just like planking any other boat. You just remember, you have to lay it out from the inside.' And that's true, because of all the bevels involved. Jim showed me how to do it, and it worked like a charm."

"That's a lost trade," said Earl. It's a trade he has shared with many others, teaching boatbuilding for 26 years. In the early 1990s he helped set up a training program at a plant in Wisconsin which had a contract to supply 230-foot wooden minesweepers for the navy. "If I had to start over, I'd do it all again. It's been a good life." [33]

The 33-foot *Sharon Lee,* for Lewis Morris of Bremerton, Washington, was one of six boats built to Plan No. 1082 by Swanson's Boat Works in 1946. One of the sister ships was *Dar-Jo,* and another was *Aunee-Al,* built by Swanson shipwrights Orrin and Al Sande, who went on to establish Sande Boat Works on the north shore of the Hood Canal. After Lewis Morris died, *Sharon Lee* was purchased by Clare and Ruthie Hicks, and renamed *Sea Hicks.* In 1966, while cruising along the shore of Sinclair Inlet, *Sea Hicks* struck a navy barge and sank to the cabin top. The boat was salvaged and rebuilt, and sold in 1970 to Charlie and Rosie Atkinson of Port Orchard, Washington, who called her *Puget Rose.* "As love affairs go, it's been a lot like one of your basic everyday love/hate relationships, not unlike some of TV's stormy soap operas," Rosie explained in a 1989 article for *Nor'westing* magazine. "We give her a little paint and varnish, haul her out every spring and scrub and paint the hull, feed her gasoline, fresh oil when she needs it, oil her squeaks and then, after a few honeymoon years, little things began to jam up. The ship-to-shore radio gave out as did some of the wiring, the water pump was replaced several times, we are on our fourth new head, and the old Olympic Range finally rusted out and had to be junked .... Charlie almost had a coronary when he found out how much a new Olympic Range from the Everett Stove Works sells for these days!" [11]

Monk drew a modern version of the sailing vessel *Spray* for a client who had been intrigued by Joshua Slocum's famous voyage. He increased the draft; even so, it was not one of his favourite designs. "The *Spray,* not originally intended for ocean cruising, was of shallow draft, quite flat-bottomed, and otherwise not well suited for the purpose." [12] More to his liking were the 38-foot cutters *Bendora* and *Halcyon II,* designed for Ben Nickells and Maurice Green of Victoria, B.C. The two men went looking for a yard and settled on the Nicholson Boat and Lumber Works in Victoria, where legendary builder/designer Frank Fredette was employed during the late 1940s. Gordon Nickells, son of Ben Nickells, remembered watching Frank Fredette at work. "Frank would cut the planks — he'd take these long beautiful pieces of yellow cedar and he'd bounce them and walk them through the saw, and they'd put them on the boat and hardly need to plane them, they fit so well." [13]

Bendora was launched in 1947 and *Halcyon II* followed in 1948, both vessels powered with "heavy duty luggers," four cylinder Gray marine gas engines. They had double berths forward, with the galley, head, and navigation table amidships, and settees aft. Jeune Brothers of Victoria made the first sets of sails, and the boats were raced extensively by their owners, both of whom served as commodores of the Royal Victoria Yacht Club.

Plan No. 1082, Puget Rose, *by Seattle artist Jack Pumphrey. "Our old 33-foot bridge-deck cruiser is a small part of a saga about six men with moderate incomes who wanted to go cruising on Puget Sound, but couldn't afford a luxury yacht. They didn't have the kind of credit at the bank to whip in there and borrow the money, so they did the next best thing: they bootlegged the design from the guy who bought the original plans.*

"The six shipyard workers set out to find a boatbuilder who they could work alongside, to save some money on labor costs. They found their boatbuilder in Gus Swanson of Shelton, Washington, (then in his 80s) who agreed to supply the basic materials for the hulls for $1,950 apiece. Gus said they could work with him to do the finishing and they could take care of their own mechanical work.*

"Even at that low price, the six men had to cut costs in other ways. As a result of their money saving methods, one of the would-be yachtsmen and his sons launched a successful boatbuilding business. The others? Well, let's just say they had more fun than a barrel of Monks!" Rosie Atkinson, author of numerous boating magazine articles during three decades of cruising local waters. [34] (COURTESY OF ROSIE ATKINSON)

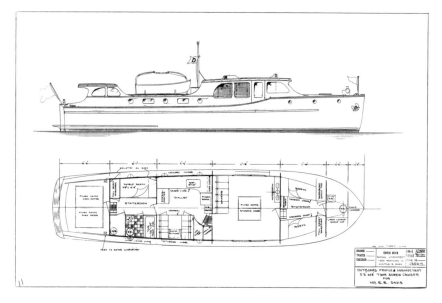

above: The Admiral Boat Company supplied Monk-designed, 12-foot skiffs to Sears-Roebuck during the late 1940s. (COURTESY OF EARL WAKEFIELD)

left: Plan No. 1350, 53-foot twin-screw cruiser for E. Davis. (COURTESY OF ED MONK JR.)

Gordon Nickells, also a past commodore, and his wife Pat cruised and raced *Bendora* for many years. "She went to windward very well because she had a split head rig. She was really, really good ... a little hard-nosed on a reach because she had such a huge main and tall mast." [14] *Bendora* was sold in 1965, and was eventually taken offshore. *Halcyon II* had several owners after being sold by Maurice Green, and was bought in 1994 by Harry Stamhuis of Maple Bay, B.C.

McChesney Boatworks, a small firm in Tacoma, Washington, built several 25-foot sloops during the early 1940s. They started working on one for the McChesney family, although progress was slow, and when the sloop was finally launched in 1953 she was christened *Happy Day*. She was double-ended with a full keel and iron ballast, Alaska cedar marine plywood on sawn oak frames, standing headroom in the galley, and mahogany trim throughout. George and Betty Hansen of Olympia, Washington, bought the boat in 1967 and began an extensive refit, renaming her *Tinka*, after all the tinkering that brought her up to shape. The Universal two cycle engine was overhauled, the foredeck was raised slightly to give more headroom, and a rub rail/bulwark was added, "to provide better footing forward and to subdue the fullness of the reverse sheer." [15] The Hansen family kept *Tinka* for 18 years and put 20,000 miles under her keel. In 1994 she was bought by Robert L. "Bob" Stewart of Port McNeill, B.C., and renamed *Laughing Otter*. Bob described her as the best sailing boat he had ever been in — after a lifetime at it, especially in light airs. He added, ruefully, "It has been said that not even the world's best designers can come up with a good-looking vessel with reverse sheer. Sad, but true, I think." [16] His intention was to set off for his home on the northern inside coast of Vancouver Island, but he did not have much confidence in the engine, which was close to 50 years old. He gave *Laughing Otter* to his friend Bill Szabo of Bellingham, Washington, and sure enough, "In September, 1996, the old Atomic 2 gave out. A hole about the size of a peach in her block did her in." The engine was removed, cleaned up, and saved to become part of a local historical display. "She is a fine vessel," reported Bill. "Very tender, goes best in ten to 15 knots of wind with full main and genoa. I am a cautious mariner and don't push her too hard, but we have been out in 30 to 40 knot winds and she was maneuverable and making headway with a reefed main and storm jib." [17]

Bob Stewart previously owned the gaff sloop *Duck*, which had an unusual cockpit layout; like *Laughing Otter*, the lockers consisted of open shelves on each side of the cockpit, with the seats built over top. She was 20 feet long on deck, "almost certainly pre-World War II, carvel-plank on steamed

Halcyon II, built in 1948. (COURTESY OF HARRY STAMHUIS)

In October 1947, Bendora *was launched at the Esquimalt drydock and towed to Esquimalt harbour for the winter, where her rigging and interior were completed by owner Ben Nickells.* (COURTESY OF GORDON NICKELLS)

Bendora, sister ship to Halcyon II, *"auxiliary cutters" built at the Nicholson yard in Victoria, B.C. Maurice Green, who operated a Victoria lumber yard, talked his good friend Ben Nickells into building a boat. Both men owned power boats at the time, but Maurice was looking around for a sailboat that would meet his needs. "We worked out the general specifications on the kitchen table," recalled Maurice, in his 90s. "Then we tossed a coin to see who would go to Seattle to meet with Ed Monk. I won." At Monk's office, "Ed pointed to a lot of half-models on the wall. I saw one and said, 'That looks like the general idea,' and he said he would come up with the plans, which he did. Ed was an honourable man to do business with, and the story of these boats was a happy story."* [(35)] (COURTESY OF GORDON NICKELLS)

above: Halcyon II. (COURTESY OF HARRY STAMHUIS)

left: Bendora. (COURTESY OF GORDON NICKELLS)

frames, quite full ended, moderately heavy, round bottom full length, no external ballast keel." [18] This was one of several designs described by Monk as "the young man's boat," the next step forward from the Flattie and the Snipe. "Every one of these originals have in actual performance shown themselves to be able and successful little boats, and in the new designs, the various characteristics, such as dimensions, speed, stability, etc., have been worked out in accordance with what is known in naval architecture as Froude's Law Of Comparison. The builder is thus assured that, built according to plans, his boat will not be a disappointment." [19]

Although Monk was responsible for all of Grandy's stock production designs, he moved his office from the Grandy yard after the war and became the first tenant in a new building on the Seattle waterfront, the Marina

Laughing Otter, ex-Tinka, ex-Happy Day, launched at McChesney Boatworks, Tacoma, in 1953. "A beloved boat," recalled George and Betty Hansen of Olympia, Washington, owners from 1967 to 1985. "The reversed sheer made for a very roomy 25-foot double-ender. The doghouse allowed standing headroom in the galley. Lots of light down below, and the 'windshield' allowed watch-keeping from a position next to the warm woodstove." [36] (COURTESY OF GEORGE AND BETTY HANSEN)

Mart. The move ensured that he had a good working relationship with local builders — including Blanchard, Jensen, Franck, Forder, Jones-Goodall, and Nordlund — and many others throughout the northwest. Monk commissioned Grandy to build a new cruiser for his own use, *Alerion*, which followed the two versions of *Western Maid*. Forty-two feet long with a single 160 hp Kermath gas engine, *Alerion* was capable of 20 mph.

True to his modest beginnings, Monk was always available to "backyard" builders. Don Sandall, an Edmonds, Washington, dentist whose father had built the "Fisherman" runabout, remembered visiting him in 1948. Don was looking for plans for his own runabout, and Monk suggested a modification of Plan No. 230, 19½ feet long. "It was my first serious effort at boatbuilding, and it served us well on Puget Sound and the Gulf Islands. Whenever I got hung up on the building process, I would visit Ed and he'd straighten me out. Even offered to drop by to see if he could help." [20] In 1965 Don visited Monk once more, for an 18-foot lapstrake design with a small cuddy cabin. He built the boat with the help of his friend Ralph Sorenson and used it for over 30 years of summer cruising, heading north as far as Desolation Sound.

Allan Boatworks of Kelso, Washington, built *Cheryl Lee*, a custom, 45-foot tri-cabin cruiser, for Dr. Lewis Carpenter in 1948. Dr. Carpenter added a flying bridge to Monk's specifications in 1965, and kept the boat for another ten years. Second owner Paul Scott repowered the boat in 1978, changing from twin gas engines to Bedford diesels. The next owner, Margaret Auld, changed the boat's name to *Sea Rose III*. Len and Lorraine Klinger of Falkland, B.C., bought *Sea Rose III* in 1989 and closed in the flying bridge, making for a very dry, comfortable boat.

The McKay and Cormack yard in Victoria found a steady market for their attractive, mid-size cruisers; the 30-foot *Jericho* was named after the Vancouver beach, and was the type of boat that Monk envisioned for the average family, with a full galley, dinette, lots of storage, and a spacious forward cabin. The 292 GM Crusader engine produced a cruising speed of nine knots. For convenience under way there were two steering stations — one inside the main cabin, and one in the cockpit; a third was added when the command bridge was built. *Jericho* was bought by Steve and Susi Jorgensen of Sidney, B.C., in 1993.

Robert Harris of Vancouver built *Lady Ann II*: 29 feet long with a nine-foot beam, cedar-planked on oak frames, fir plywood deck and cabin top, and mahogany cabin. The engine, originally a 100 hp flathead V-8, was replaced by a 165 hp Ford V-8. John and Anne King of Victoria, B.C., purchased *Lady Ann II* in 1992 and then spent 99% of their time refastening the hull, replacing the transom and main cabin, including part of the roof and some

Carvel-planked runabout built of Alaska red cedar by Don Sandall of Edmonds, Washington, in 1948. Hard-chine, semi-V bottom — which "rode smoother in rough water and cut the water softer" than the 18-foot round-bottom lapstrake runabout that Don built next. [37] (COURTESY OF DON SANDALL)

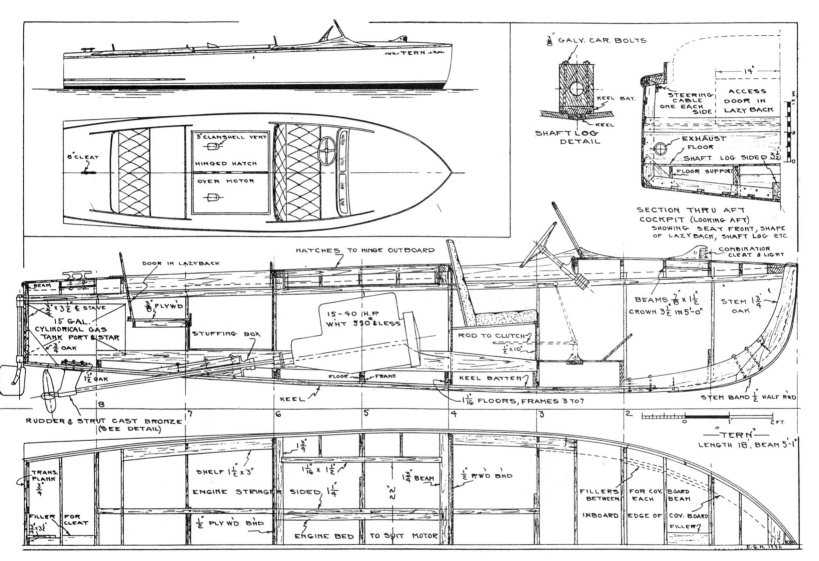

"Tern," 18-foot runabout from Monk's first book, Small Boat Building.

Loueda, *a best-selling design after the war. Length 32 ft., beam 9 ft., solid Honduras mahogany cabin, red cedar planking below the waterline and yellow cedar above. Built by H. Snider of Vancouver, B.C., in 1947 and restored by Elmer "Buck" Buckingham, who owned* Loueda *from 1987 to 1997.* (COURTESY OF ELMER BUCKINGHAM)

The Sweet Sound, *originally* Heather, *built by Grandy for Alex McCallum in 1948. Length 34 ft., beam 11 ft., draft 4 ft., powered by a 327 Chrysler V-8. Sedan cruiser with V-berth forward; main cabin, galley, and head on one level. "A very snug boat in all kinds of weather," reported owners Carl and Barbara Montford of Seattle, Washington. "We have cruising heat, dockside heat, and on-the-hook heat. It is easy to tell that the boat was designed in the northwest for cruising in the northwest."* [38] (Courtesy of Carl Montford)

Norm Collins of Seattle, Washington, presented Monk with sketches for a 37-foot centre-cockpit cruiser. Built by Ed Sundquist of Ballard, Washington, in 1947, "*Mimi* was great," Norm recalled in 1997. "The central cockpit idea immediately graduated into the elevated bridges so prevalent today. Either way, we are now getting more vision and good sea air, although the original motive for the central cockpit was to prevent the kids from falling overboard, unseen." Other boats with lines similar to *Mimi* soon followed: *Tanda*, for Ed Oban, and *Chevron*, for Jerry Bryant. The Collins family cruised in *Mimi* for many years; she was later owned by Bob and Nita Ostlund, Seattle. [39]

roof beams, replacing the decks and several planks and frames, and installing new through-hull fittings, exhaust system, salt-water cooling, fresh-water cooling, wiring, ignition, battery box and batteries, instruments, cleats, bollards, horn, and lights. The window glass was replaced, the cabin interior was stripped, and John King built new hand rails, mast, rub rails, bulwarks and trim. "Probably many details left out or forgotten in this list," commented John, "but this turned out to be a 'bad case' and there is no going back." [21] Fully restored in 1998, with the assistance of Mark Aitken of Victoria General Marine, *Lady Ann II* was ready for her first cruise in six years.

Harverdor, 34 feet long, was built by H. Bursey of Port Mellon, B.C. "Handles beautifully and is a joy to be on," [22] reported fourth owners Wayne and Chris Robinson of Gibsons, B.C. The boat was renamed *Crusader VII* and refurbished in the 1980s, with maintenance simplified by painting over the brightwork. The Chrysler Royal gas engine was upgraded to an 85 hp Chrysler Nissan diesel, giving a cruising speed of eight knots.

In 1949 Leslie Horner of Vancouver built the 35-foot *Rondavel*, a sedan cruiser outfitted with twin Chevrolet Mercruiser engines. She was later called *Lady Audrey*, and participated in numerous local regattas. Her original name restored, she was purchased in 1985 by Gerry Flowers of Maple Bay, B.C.

Hukiliu, 36 feet long, with 11½ foot beam and three-foot draft, was built for Fred Fawcett in Seattle and purchased by Barb and Dan Moldenhauer of Shelton, Washington, in 1990. "We don't really own them," said Dan, referring to his years of caring for classic boats. "We just keep them in good health to pass them on, hopefully, to the next generation." [23]

Eric Philbrook of Victoria, B.C., built the 39-foot bridge-deck cruiser *Bonnie Lou* in the backyard of his Victoria home in 1951. Proceeds from the 1955 sale of the boat went towards starting Philbrook's Shipyard, which became a successful business on Tsehum Harbour in Sidney, B.C. *Bonnie Lou* was renamed *Lady Madge*, then *Tzinquaw II*, and returned to the Philbrook family in 1994, purchased by Eric Philbrook's granddaughter, Sue Wilson, and her husband, Chris Wilson, of Sidney. The engine, a straight eight cylinder Chrysler Royal, produced a maximum speed of 13 knots and a cruising speed of 11 knots.

"What kind of boats are people waiting to build or buy — how much different from pre-war designs and sizes?" Monk had asked, in 1944. "The stock design will no doubt come back with a bang and pretty well monopolize the field up to about 40 feet, with its peak around 30 feet." [24] With his name now recognized throughout the northwest, he was well positioned to contribute to the renewed success of both large and small boat yards, many of which had been in the same families for several generations.

Duffy, *35-foot sedan cruiser built by Adams Boat Company in 1950 for Eugene and Elaine Kidd of Seattle. Cruising speed of nine knots, with a 200 hp Marine Power V-6, new in 1996. Although very sound when purchased by Mike and Gwen Byrne of Shelton, Washington, in 1992,* Duffy *underwent a restoration not untypical for its age: painted surfaces stripped and varnished; new fuel and water tanks, holding tank and pump; rewiring; new engine and transmission, throttle and gear shift cables and controls; added seating and storage; interior head liner replaced; upgraded electronics; a Dickinson stove in the galley, for cooking and heat.* [40] (COURTESY OF MIKE AND GWEN BYRNE)

*H*ukiliu, 1950, received a new Volvo diesel engine in 1996. Owners Dan and Barb Moldenhauer also gave her a new name, *T'u T'u Baqs*, the Makah Indian word for loon.

"We both enjoy the Northwest Indian culture so we wanted an Indian name. I phoned the curator at the Makah Indian Museum in Neah Bay and asked if she would send me a list of Indian words that describe fowl, fish, or wildlife. She said she would be very happy to do so. I asked if I could send some money to pay for this. She said sure, two dollars would be enough.

"Weeks, then months went by. The check had cleared the bank. (I know, it's only two dollars.) I called again and spoke with the same woman. She was very nice and very apologetic. Then she explained that they had just started making a written language and didn't realize it would take so long. She said it would probably be a few more months. 'No problem,' I said. 'Whenever, would be great.' I was just so pleased for them and us.

"Months go by, and the work on the boat is almost complete. Dan doesn't do all the restoration work but the work gets done because of him. He nurtures these 'grand old ladies' like he would care for his grandmother if she were alive today.

"It was some time later we received a package from the Museum. It contained several lists of names/words for fish, fowl, etc. It also included a drawing and explanation of how to speak Makah. Then, too, was a cassette tape with Helma Ward saying the Makah pronunciation and the other woman saying the English word. It's wonderful ... they were so generous to us. (You can bet I sent another check, and it wasn't just two dollars!)" Barb Moldenhauer. [41]

T'u T'u Baqs, *formerly* Hukiliu. (COURTESY OF BARB MOLDENHAUER)

T'u T'u Baqs. (Courtesy of Barb Moldenhauer)

above: First boat built by Philbrook's — Bonnie Lou *(later* Tzinquaw II*) — carvel-planked, red cedar hull over bent-oak frames, mahogany topsides, single gas engine — standard construction for 1950.* (COURTESY OF VIC GRIFFIN)

right: Bonnie Lou, *launched at Esquimalt, B.C., in 1951.* (COURTESY OF CHRIS AND SUE WILSON)

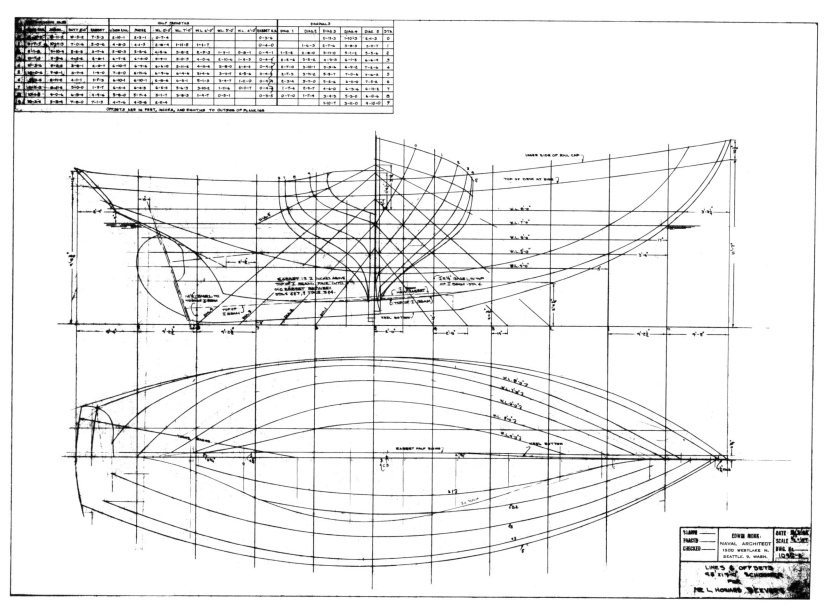

Plan No. 1096, lines and offsets of schooner, length 46 ft., beam 14 ft., for Howard Seevers. (COURTESY OF ED MONK JR.)

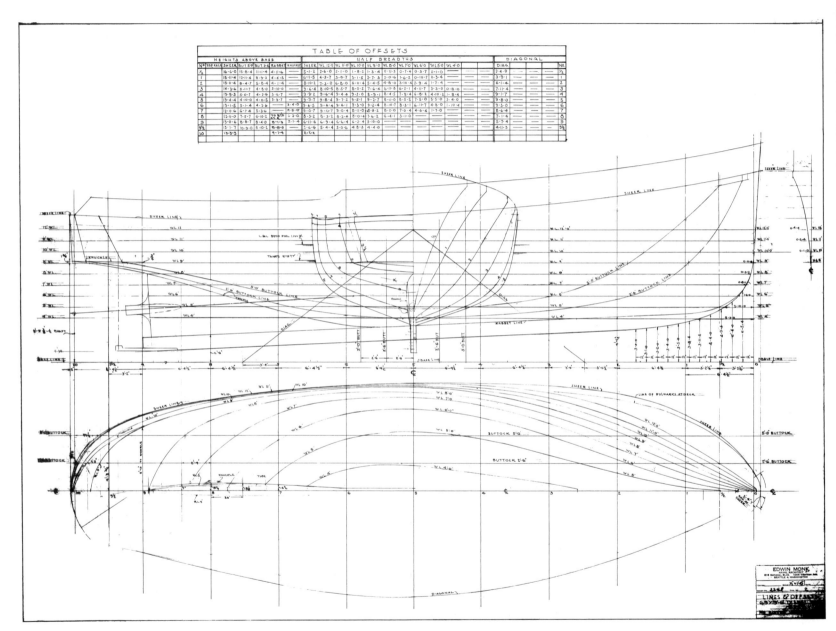

*Plan No. 2248, lines and offsets of diesel tug, length 65 ft., beam
19 ½ ft., for B. Halvorsen. (*COURTESY OF ED MONK JR.*)*

CHAPTER FIVE

"SOMETHING A LITTLE NEW IN HULL DESIGN"

B Y THE EARLY 1950s the boating industry was responding to the wave of optimism sweeping over the country; as Monk had foreseen, thousands of middle-class buyers were discovering the pleasures of family cruising. Although most of the boats were simple by present standards, they offered amenities — such as upholstered seating, carpeting, and "decorated" cabins — previously unavailable except in luxurious yachts. Marinas were expanding, the U.S. Power Squadron was offering free classes in Piloting and Small Boat Handling, and clubhouses were going up from San Diego to Vancouver to accommodate the new yachting public.

These progressive times, with customers in abundance, were an opportunity for designers to experiment with hull performance and the layout of their boats. Previously, there had been little choice; the large, heavy motor was placed amidships for stability, and accommodations were designed around it. In 1896 when *Montana* was built, the first gasoline-propelled pleasure boat in lower Puget Sound, it was powered by a one cylinder, two hp Union engine with a six-inch bore and stroke — weighing 1,500 pounds. "Today," Monk wrote in 1953, "with forced feed lubrication, the V-drive motor and remote control, the power plant can be placed almost anywhere. Successful cruisers have been turned out where the motor almost touches the stem and we are all familiar with the V-drive with the motor close to the transom. These innovations are chiefly responsible for the many excellent and varied arrangements found in today's power cruisers." [1] From the same basic hull, four main styles emerged: the sedan, the flying- or open-bridge, the bridge-deck, and the after-cabin cruiser, each with its benefits, depending on the owner's taste and intentions. "One ... client was firmly convinced that the motor should be in the bow, as far forward as possible. The theory was that this was the least usable and

"A round 1933-34 Chrysler came out with Chrysler Marine engines. They had the little engine which they called the Ace, six cylinders, 90 hp, then they had the Crown, six cylinders, 120 hp, and this was really some engine. Then there were the Kermaths, which were starting to be converted to marine use. Back in the old days there were the Redwing engines and the Hercules engines. The heavy Easthope engines and Vivian engines used to plug along at slow revolutions, about six to eight knots. The bigger boats had heavy duty diesels that were massive — Atlas Imperials and Cooper Bessemers and those types. To get 300 hp, the engine was about ten feet long and five feet high, from the bottom of the base to the top of the cylinders, with six pistons in it, about 10½ inches bore, and that thing weighed pretty close to two or three tons. And that was just 300 hp. They found out after the war that they could take 500 hp out of an engine that weighed 2,000 pounds, whereas in the old days 500 hp would weigh about five tons. They started to build faster boats, and they thought they had a speedboat when it was doing 12 to 15 knots. They started to use the automotive engine, and converted it to marine. And they put two to one transmissions on, then three to one, and so on, so they had the revolutions to get their torque out of them, with the reduction gear, so they could have a bigger wheel. Because with a small wheel, a direct drive, as soon as you get over 1,500 revs, a lot of efficiency is lost. Now we're getting 300 hp out of something that weighs just 1,200 pounds. This is where yachting has blossomed — putting in the horsepower to get the speed. Everyone's in a hurry, these days." Vic Griffin. [42]

Capital City Yacht Club rendezvous at Genoa Bay, B.C., 1951, with
Hi-Seas *and* Bonnie Lou. (COURTESY OF VIC GRIFFIN)

Adventurer, *Plan No. 1399, built for Otis Harlan in 1948. Monk also designed Harlan's 80-foot, long-range cruiser* Adventurer II, *in the 1960s.* (Ray Krantz, courtesy of Ed Monk Jr.)

In their quest for improved performance, builders and designers were experimenting with the use of a wedge — "an addition or protuberance secured to the bottom of a boat at the transom." The action of the wedge was to exert an upward pressure which would provide a lift on the transom. Theoretically, there would be an increase in speed and a better running angle — or, a small sacrifice in speed for a more comfortable running angle. "There are two factors which upset pure theory so that in practice the pressure does not actually increase this way .... These factors are resurgence and wake, which are actually related to each other." Monk carried out a series of tests to put the matter to rest. Would a wedge help? "If the running angle is four degrees or less, it will not." To be effective, he deduced, the wedge should be the full width of the transom. [43]

"The spirit of adventure does still survive in most of us .... Eventually an urge to see new places, touch into strange harbors and anchor in new coves prompts us to look around to see where we might turn, where there are no 'Private Property' signs and where anchorages are not filled with boats and water skiers." Ed Monk. [44]

desirable portion of the boat, a hatch overhead would make for its easy removal and with the steering position on the after side of the engine room bulkhead, the problem of controls would be simplicity itself. Placing the major weight so far forward presented a difficult problem in weight distribution; nevertheless the boat was finally designed and built and, surprisingly enough, turned out quite well." [2]

In Monk's opinion, the forward part of a boat should be used for sleeping quarters, the narrow floor room and widening hull at berth height suiting this purpose. Here is where the skipper should sleep while at anchor, he advised, to be aware of changes in weather. The flying bridge was an asset, with the skipper keeping watch for "the great amount of debris afloat ... deadheads, logs, mill scraps, etc. 'If you can't see 'em, you can't hit 'em' may apply to baseball, but just the opposite is true on the water. Visibility is best in the flying bridge ... and poorest in the after cabin boat." Living aboard *Nan* had given Monk a thorough respect for good heating and ventilation systems, and for the well-being of the cook: "The galley had best not be so located that she sees only the masts, tree tops and the sky." The ideal steering position — again based on his own experience — allowed "one eye on the boat and the other on the juveniles. Every family probably has had a bad moment or two when someone asks 'where's Freddie,' and then a feeling of great relief when he is found asleep, or perhaps hiding in a locker." [3]

Monk's own boat, *Alerion*, was a single-screw sedan cruiser with an open bridge, "something a little new in hull design, the bottom being monohedron and the hull of fairly light construction." [4] The term "monohedron" describes a hull with constant deadrise and was first used by naval architect Lindsay Lord. "Deadrise" refers to the angle that sections of the hull make with the ground — with a deep V boat having lots of deadrise and a flat-bottom skiff having none. In his 1992 book *The Nature Of Boats*, Dave Gerr explained, "These days, most planing hulls have nearly constant deadrise in their run," [5] unlike early designs, which had hulls as flat as possible aft, based on the reasoning that "a flat underbody generates the most planing lift for a given horsepower." [6] Although this was true, it meant that the deadrise forward needed to be very large, to prevent pounding. "Accordingly, these designers started forward with tremendous deadrise (a sharp entry) and decreased the deadrise gradually and steadily as they went aft, until — all the way at the stern, there was no deadrise at all." [7] The resulting flat bottom at the transom had a detrimental effect on water flow under the vessel, reducing speed. Hulls with varying deadrise, called "warped bottom," were gradually giving way to faster-performing hulls with constant deadrise, and the term monohedron came into general use. Monk experimented with the new hull shape prior to commissioning *Alerion*, using models built by Earl Wakefield. In 1948, *Yachting* magazine featured a 30-foot monohedron stock production design by Lindsay Lord, acquired by yards across North America and Europe. The appeal was speed: a pair of eight cylinder Packard engines drove Lord's boat at 28 mph.

Taking his own boat cruising was Monk's best chance to test his ideas, and in the summer of 1952 he set off with his family for the west coast of Vancouver Island. They were travelling with Ersal Davis and his wife on the Monk-designed *Chilton*, and Dick Taylor and his family on *Como Reto*. The 54-foot *Chilton*, heavily constructed with two V-drive motors, had a bathtub on board "which proved an asset to the entire company." [8] They left Seattle on July 22 — a month too late, Monk noted — encountering fog, then brisk northwest winds. Monk's wife and his eldest daughter became seasick, for the first time ever, and the fog continued all the way to Barkley Sound. *Chilton* nosed up on an unmarked reef while checking out an anchorage in the Broken Group. "A good argument for a shoe on every keel," commented Monk, when he saw the jagged slivers on *Chilton*'s ironbark shoe. After clearing customs at Bamfield, the second group of American pleasure boats of the season, they explored the inlet all the way to Port Alberni, where Monk was interviewed by the local newspaper. They set out for Tofino, again in heavy fog, turning in towards land at the sound of the horn on the lighthouse at Lennard Island.

During the trip the three boats were frequently anchored in a swell, and climbing in and out of the dinghy gave everyone an appreciation for *Alerion*'s boarding platform and transom door. "Like everything new," said Monk, "this met a lot of sales resistance at first, principally because it was thought dangerous in a following sea." [9] On their way home, heading back down the coast, "here I had a good opportunity to observe the transom door in a fairly steep high following sea, and watch it from the cockpit for long periods. Once in a while a little water seeped through the cracks and ran out the scuppers, but it was surprising how the stern rose to a swell. You would swear the next high one would come near the top, but it just seemed to vanish and pass under the boat." [10]

One of the first Puget Sound companies to capitalize on the demand for affordable, factory-built boats was Tollycraft Yachts, founded by Monk's friend Tolly Tollefson in 1952. Monk drew up plans for the Tollycraft 14-, 16-, 18-, and 21-footers — to be built of plywood, with fibreglass overlay. "As far as I'm concerned," said Tollefson, "as a small-boat designer, he was probably the best in the country. He was very

The naval architect analyzes the "slam": Cruising up the Strait of Juan de Fuca, *Alerion* meets a nasty sea "almost square, high and steep. Our boat is quite sharp forward," reported Monk, "nevertheless, she came down once in a while with a terrific slam.

"We are all vitally interested in boat performance. We may note the fairly sharp forward sections and decide that this one will never pound. However, we should take into consideration the fact that there is always some area of nearly flat or even concave surface and that in an irregular sea the force of the water may come from almost any direction. The center of gravity in a modern power cruiser is well aft of amidship. The bow runs out over the top of a steep sea; then as all support is suddenly withdrawn it drops with almost alarming rapidity upon a decidedly irregular surface. The right contacts for a good slam are certain to occur." [45]

"One of Ed Monk's greatest assets was his knowledge of boating in the Pacific Northwest. Ed designed layouts for the sometimes very wet weather, and hence more inside space, and less outside deck spaces. I have always credited Ed with two innovative northwest features on his boats, namely, the swim [grid] or rear boarding platform, and the rear gate from the cockpit to the boarding platform.

"In the northwest, once we leave major areas, all boating is done by anchoring in secluded areas, when the dinghy is brought to the stern, and we get out the gate, onto the platform, and into either the dinghy or swimming! Very simple, but terrific idea." Robert Gibson, owner of four Monk-designed boats, all named *Gibson Gal*. [46]

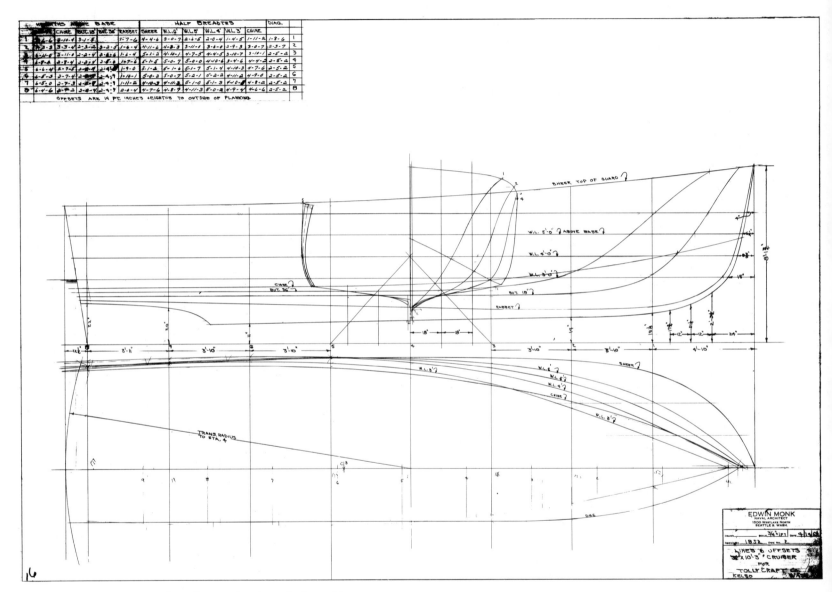

Plan No. 1852, lines and offsets of cruiser, length 32 ft., beam 10 ft. 3 in., for Tollycraft Company. (COURTESY OF ED MONK JR.)

private and soft-spoken and he would never argue with his customers. He would listen to all their ideas, and he wouldn't agree or disagree, he might mention some factors that might enter into it, but he was never absolutely positive. He never raised his voice." As Tollycraft outgrew their site in Kelso, Washington, Tollefson looked around for a larger property, but was unable to get mortgage money. He decided to sell stock in his company, to raise cash. "Ed Monk heard about this, and he bought shares in Tollycraft which he held right up till the time I sold out. Mrs. Monk said, after he died, 'Ed told me never to sell that.' " The new plant was built in 1959, on 15 acres of land near the airport in Kelso. The Tollycraft line proved extremely popular and continued expanding; by 1962 many of the boats were built entirely of fibreglass. "The other thing that was remarkable about Ed," added Tollefson, "was that you never felt you were overcharged for his services. Because of his reputation, he probably could have got double the hourly wage that he charged. He had his own expertise and I don't think anyone would question it. He was revered — because he was such a gentleman." (11)

Commissions for fishing boats continued through the 1950s, many of them taking shape one at a time in backyards along the coast. Chappell's Boat Works on Lulu Island, Richmond, B.C., launched a 38-foot troller in 1950, *Mid Century Star*, for Stan Kondrat of Port Alice on northern Vancouver Island. Stan's son, Ron Kondrat, took over the boat when his father died, and used it for many years. The fast day troller *Lenita*, launched at Port Alberni Shipyard for fisherman Jack Kampe in 1952, was later bought by Ron's brother, Gary Kondrat. *Lenita* was 34 feet 8 inches long, with a ten-foot beam and five-foot draft. The original engine was a Chrysler Crown, replaced by a 380 cubic inch Ford diesel. *Lenita*'s semi-displacement hull was similar to an east-coast lobster boat, only with a deeper, sharper bow and rounded chine at the stern. "The general idea," explained Ron Kondrat, "is to run out to the fishing grounds early, put in as long a day as practical, then run back to harbour to deliver the fish fresh the same day. *Lenita* is lightly constructed, for speed, but trolling poles and extra rigging slow her down." (12)

Years of working with offshore fishermen had furthered Monk's interest in developing plans for a "troller-type cruiser" which would be safe and comfortable at sea. In 1952, the 42-foot *Scaup* was launched at Clark Brothers boat yard in Brentwood Bay, B.C., marking another milestone in Monk's career. She was commissioned by Alberta businessman J.M. Taylor, who spent summers in nearby Sidney and had watched the commercial trollers taking shape in the Clark Brothers yard. Taylor asked Clark

Sea Sea Rider — *28-foot Tollycraft "Voyager" (1966), bronze fastenings, marine fir plywood with fibreglass overlay. Warm, mahogany-trimmed interior, 318 Chrysler engine, with a speed of 18 knots. Owned since 1996 by Cam Elder and Rich Karvonen of Everett, Washington.* (COURTESY OF CAM ELDER)

"Due to the nature of their work, trollers must go to sea, often for a week or more at a time. They must provide a seakindly and seaworthy home and work platform. Trollers seldom catch great amounts of fish and therefore don't need a fat shape to carry the load, thereby allowing a more efficient and seakindly shape than many other fish boats. These characteristics as well as their salty style lend themselves well to the offshore cruiser." Ed Monk. (47)

West-coast troller *Mid Century Star*, Plan No. 1303: length 38 ft., beam 11 ft. 8 in., draft 6 ft. Yellow cedar decks and hull planking, fir stringers, oak ribs. Started out with a Chrysler Royal engine; a six cylinder Volvo Penta MD-50A diesel was installed in 1966 and rebuilt in 1992, after 50,000 hours. Two-inch shaft, and a 32-inch by 22-inch three blade propeller. Commissioned by Stan Kondrat, later owned by his son, Ron Kondrat, of Vancouver, B.C. "My father met Edwin Monk in Winter Harbour at the old general store dock. I assume it would have been after 1957 as the bulwarks had been extended to the end of the wheelhouse. Edwin Monk had been travelling around Vancouver Island in his own cruiser and had tied up across the dock, adjacent to my father's boat in Winter Harbour. He had recognized the hull and chatted with my father about the boat and other related subjects."

After many years of fishing off the west coast of Vancouver Island, Ron Kondrat had a great affection for *Mid Century Star*. "Easy driving displacement hull, built as a combination salmon troller/halibut longliner with a bait hatch and large fish hold. Hull has very nice lines — all curves, large crown main deck matched with crown on stern timbers and wheelhouse roof. Appears to have some tumblehome in hull. Timbered stern, gumwood stem. Modifications to the original plan were: more flare in bow section; the hull raised by one plank, to enhance packing ability; wheelhouse raised for more headroom and also for enhanced visibility. Bow cleat and portholes come from the *Morgan*, an old rumrunner.

"The boat once took a severe roll with all the halibut gear on deck, and no ice, in a tide rip under Lions Gate bridge but still recovered after lying on her side. After prepared with six tons of ice in halibut format she has proved to be an excellent sea boat operating in some very miserable conditions — because if bad weather comes up, you have to stay…

Residence Phone HEmlock 4415

Office Phone GArfield 7907

EDWIN MONK
LORNE GARDEN

Edwin Monk

NAVAL ARCHITECTS
1500 WESTLAKE N.   SEATTLE 9
November 22, 1949

Mr. S. Kondrat
Port Alice, B.C.

Dear Mr. Kondrat:

We are glad you are interested in the 38' Troller design No. 1303.

We have just talked to a boat builder yesterday who showed us pictures of one of these models, and both he and the owner were extremely well satisfied with the performance of the boat during the past fishing season.

Cost of plans are $80.00. Should you have any difficulty sending money to this country, you can send the Canadian money order to us and we will deposit it in Canada to our Canadian account.

Sincerely yours,

Lorne Garde
LORNE GARDEN

LG:me

PLEASURE AND COMMERCIAL CRAFT   WOOD AND STEEL

(COURTESY OF RON KONDRAT)

out to recover your gear or lose it all. As a troller she has good seakeeping ability — has received many compliments on how well the boat rides in a sea way. She fits the bill nicely as a fishing and packing boat with somewhat cramped and spartan living accommodations. Consumes no more than three Imperial gallons per hour, and usually less. Being loaded or empty seems to have no effect on speed or fuel consumption." [48]

above left and right: West-coast troller Mid Century Star (Courtesy of Ron Kondrat)

right: Echo, *35-foot gillnetter, Plan No. 1925.* (Courtesy of Ed Monk Jr.)

QT, *out of San Francisco.* (COURTESY OF ED MONK JR.)

Brothers if they would build him a similar boat, to be used for pleasure cruising to Alaska. Stan Clark went to Seattle and consulted with Monk. The drawings for *Scaup*, a "heavy cruiser," were completed by Monk and his partner, Lorne Garden.

Scaup was sold to Taylor's cruising companion, Colonel Rolly Bull, then sold in 1960 to Doug Marshall and his family, who were also friends with Taylor. The Marshalls owned *Scaup* for 25 years and had Clark Brothers add the flying bridge. Paravane stabilizers were installed in 1970, 20-foot poles supported by an aluminum A-frame, a system which worked very well, resulting in a 70% reduction in roll. John West purchased *Scaup* in 1988 and maintained her immaculate condition; during the 1990s she was the committee boat for Victoria's Classic Boat Festival.

Scaup was followed by the 40-foot *Skookum Maru*, launched at G. Kugge Boatworks in Kobe, Japan. Owners Gordon and Blanche Rogers of Berkeley, California, asked Monk to design *Skookum Maru* after several seasons of chartering in the northwest. *Skookum* is a Chinook word meaning strong, and *maru* is Japanese for circle, a name often used for Japanese ships because of a ship's similarity to a circle, a complete entity. The Rogers enjoyed 30 years of cruising the B.C. and Alaska coasts, often in the company of friends. *Skookum Maru* carried two nine-foot Davidson dinghies as tenders, and had a Dickinson oil stove for cooking and heat. She was sold to Jeanette Lucrisia of Seattle, Washington, and has undergone restoration by Richard and Kim Asia, also of Seattle, her owners since 1995.

Skookum Maru and another heavy displacement vessel, *Scottish Lass*, were featured in the first edition of Robert P. Beebe's *Voyaging Under Power*, a book which led the discussion of "the quest for a seagoing motor boat to 'cross oceans with speed and dispatch.' " [13] Beebe had designed for himself the 60-foot *Passagemaker*, built and launched in Singapore in the early 1960s. *Passagemaker* carried her owner across 6,000 miles of ocean, and was used as a basis for Beebe's many years of research into the safety and performance of power boats at sea.

Beebe described Monk as a "pioneer in the development of the 'Northwest cruiser,' which might be characterized as having lines a step away from the true displacement hull, with modifications aft to allow speed to an S/L ratio of about 1.65." [14] The 45-foot *Scottish Lass* (renamed *Gillean*) was commissioned by Duncan MacLean of Seattle and built by Yamanaka Boat Works of Steveston, B.C., in 1962. She had a 14-foot beam and five-foot draft, and was designed to carry 1,800 pounds of ballast on her keel. "It is more for roll smoothness and peace of mind than ultimate

"The so-called 'west-coast troller' that still works all the world's waters is largely Ed Monk's design, or designed by someone influenced by his designs. You can recognize one of his boats by the short raised deck just ahead of the pilothouse. This was to give headroom going down to the forecastle where the crew's quarters were located, without giving up too much space in the pilothouse to a stairway.

"I helped build and later skippered a 46-foot Monk-designed troller chasing albacore tuna up and down the Pacific coast. I always puffed up a little when California fishermen would comment, 'Wow, look at that ... he's got one of those Northern boats!' Even on the east coast fishermen know that if they want the best, they need a Monk, preferably built on our coast out of our famous woods. That was a super sea boat. We kept fishing until the wind grew so strong it blew the lead jigs out of the water — about 70 knots." Tom Kincaid, founder of *Nor'westing* magazine. [49]

"*Scaup* has a conservative and heavy hull, with less deadrise and not as full in section as a commercial troller of the time. The forefoot is slightly cut away. A transom stern replaced the double-ended or compromise stern of the working boats. The accommodation is a small foc'sle with a single berth, a settee, and a private head. The wheelhouse is situated well forward, giving excellent visibility as the coast is prone to large amounts of drift. The wheelhouse can be closed off from the rest of the accommodation for darkened night running. The galley is a step down from the wheelhouse, with the dinette opposite. Then an aft cabin with sleeping berths." John West. [50]

above: The launching of Scaup, April 1952. Carvel-planked hull, 1¾ inch fir over bent-oak frames fastened with galvanized nails. Caulked fir decks over plywood; 400 gallons of fuel. Length 42 ft., beam 11½ ft., draft 5½ ft. The original twin Chrysler Crown M 47 engines were replaced with twin 126 hp six cylinder Volvo MD-50 diesel engines. Cruising speed 7.8 knots at 1,600 rpm, using 2½ Imperial gallons per hour. (COURTESY OF HENRY CLARK)

right: Scaup, 42-foot cruiser, Plan No. 1674. (COURTESY OF ED MONK JR.)

Scaup. (COURTESY OF HENRY CLARK)

"*Skookum Maru*, designed in 1955, is one of the earlier breed of heavy-duty cruisers, and has proven her mettle in extensive coastal cruising .... Her arrangement is interesting in that it is one of the first COHO or 'tri-cabin' type layouts, which feature separated permanent sleeping accommodations, and a central living area combining culinary, lounging, and navigational functions in one cabin. This arrangement has proved particularly popular, both because of the sleeping privacy and comfort aft for the master stateroom, and togetherness during waking hours." Ed Monk. [51]

Skookum Maru was built by G. Kugge Boatworks of Kobe, Japan, and brought across the Pacific on the deck of a steamship. Length 40 ft., beam 12 ft., draft 4½ ft., 21 gross tons. Carvel-planked hull of 1¼ inch Philippine mahogany, keyaki wood frames. Powered by GM 3-71 diesel, dry exhaust.

"A Detroit 3-71 68 hp diesel gives a cruising speed of eight knots, though the hull could absorb a bit more power for a cruising speed closer to nine knots. Fuel and water are very small by today's standards, with 350 gallons of fuel and 120 gallons of water. However, these have proven enough to take the Rogers where they want to go. Perhaps we waste too much space and money on tankage in today's coastal cruisers when we give them the capacity for the ocean crossing the owners rarely make." Ed Monk. [52]

"Designed first by ... Edwin Monk and William Garden, a type of boat began to evolve which was lighter and more economical than a true fisherman, yet offered adequate seaworthiness. 'Northwest Cruisers' they were commonly called at first, though this term has about died out today. As more and more of these boats were built, their reputation gradually became widespread and led to the sudden proliferation of vessels that today are called 'trawlers.'" Robert P. Beebe. [53]

stability," commented Monk, "though it would help in a bad beam-sea situation." [15] The Gardner 6LX diesel engine, selected for its quiet running and reliability, gave a speed of eight to nine knots using less than two gallons of fuel per hour. At least eight other boats were built to the same plan, No. 2266. Yamanaka Boat Works also built the 44-foot *Cavalier* for William Anderson of Vancouver, B.C.

Monk preferred lighter, faster boats for his own use, and by the mid-1950s he was again ready for something new — a 37-foot, flying-bridge cruiser constructed by Martin Monson's Seattle yard. The boat was named *Whim*, after the hours Monk spent discussing his latest ideas with his wife when he came home from work to the house he had built at Port Madison. *Whim*'s semi-planing, monohedron hull, both efficient and aesthetically pleasing, gave rise to many variations which were launched in the coming years. "It features a high chine forward, a straight run or buttocks aft, and a reverse to the frames at the keel. The monohedron shape also lends itself well to the round bottom boat and is perhaps the fastest boat, either V or round, for its size with moderate power." The high chine eliminated the tendency to pound; the straight buttocks made for a level riding boat without resorting to the use of wedges, and the reverse sections at the keel gave better directional stability. Extra frames were added to *Whim*'s forward section — the intermediate frames from keel to chine were doubled after the boat was planked, and fastened with glue and screws. "A fast hull must necessarily take considerable punishment, most of it forward, and it seems only logical to strengthen the boat where strength is most required." [16]

Whim had a 200 hp Chrysler Imperial V-8 gas engine, one of the first in the northwest. The boarding platform facilitated the use of an auxiliary motor for trolling and for emergencies. A small piece of wood was designed to be clamped to the platform, for attaching the motor. A five hp long-shaft motor would give about three knots cruising speed on a 40-foot boat "... which is just about right for salmon trolling. I think trolling is the hardest use, and the most abuse, the main power plant has to take." The cabin windows were sealed with a new type of rubber retainer adapted from the automotive industry, eliminating rabbetting, bedding compound, and window stops. A roomy main cabin with a large dinette accommodated guests for dinner, with the galley opposite. There were two heads: " ... a spare is like having twin engines, except that a fellow yachtsman can pass you a towline if you break down, but he can seldom lend a spare toilet." The oil stove was custom-made out of aluminum, less than half the weight of a traditional cast- and sheet-iron range. An ice-box was installed, instead

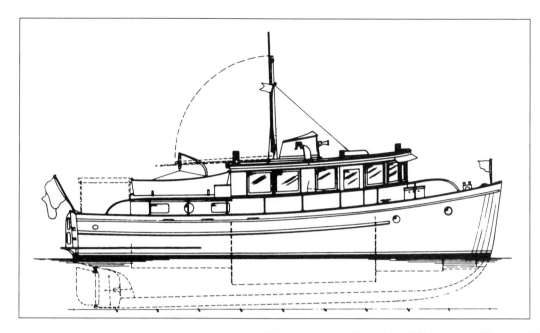

left: Profile plan for 40-foot Skookum Maru. (COURTESY OF ED MONK JR.)

below: Betty J, *length 43 ft., beam 12½ ft., draft 5 ft. Wedge-seamed hull, yellow cedar below the waterline, red cedar above, on oak frames. Double-planked gumwood for 12 inches below the waterline. GM 6-71 diesel engine, stabilizers installed in 1995. Built by Tripple and Everett Marine Ways for William Smith of Seattle in the late 1950s. A workboat-style yacht, owned by Peter Smith of Sidney, B.C. (COURTESY OF PETER SMITH)*

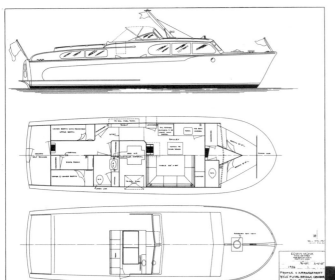

Whim, *Plan No. 1956-1, 37-foot cruiser for the Monk family.* "When the naval architect builds, or has built, a boat for his own use, he probably has more trouble making up his own mind than do his clients. It seems a human weakness to be able to tell others just what to do but to have some difficulty deciding for oneself .... There are many ideas he would like to try, ideas he hesitates to attempt on a client's boat because of prudence and the understandable reluctance of the client to try the untried. He thinks to himself, 'Well, if it doesn't work on my own boat, I don't have to tell everybody about it.' " *Ed Monk.* [54] (COURTESY OF ED MONK JR.)

Monk's daughter Judy (later Judy Wade) aboard Whim, *Port Madison.* (COURTESY OF ED MONK JR.)

of electric refrigeration requiring large batteries and a compressor. "Any saving that can be made in weight will pay for itself for the entire life of the boat and if little or no effort is made in this direction, it is almost as though one took the surplus wood and other materials and built another boat, towing it along wherever he went." The problem, he noted, was that "Yachtsmen are probably the world's greatest gadgeteers." [17] A sonic depthsounder, finally low enough in price to be affordable, was one of the few gadgets he conceded to have on board.

The launching of *Whim* was also the start of two lasting friendships for Monk — with businessman Robert "Bob" Gibson and boatbuilder George McQueen of Vancouver, B.C. Bob Gibson remembered his first meeting with Monk, "... when I journeyed from Vancouver to Seattle, and took the Bainbridge Island ferry to his home. The purpose of the visit was to take a test run on his new *Whim*, and to inspect the construction and layout. We were obviously pleased, and discussion took place, bringing about a number of changes, modifications, and in our opinion, some improvements. Ed was then instructed to proceed with the plans for our new vessel to be called *Gibson Gal*.

"By the time Ed got all the changes on the plans, it turned out to be a 38-foot vessel rather than 36-foot. Also the *Whim* had a single 200 hp Chrysler marine engine, and being a novice boat handler, at that time, I opted for the reliability of two engines — Chrysler 125 hp each — believing that two of anything is better than one! In theory, the two engines should have produced the same speed as the larger single engine, but in reality they did not, so in 1958 I took out the two Chrysler Crowns and replaced them with twin 200 hp Chrysler V-8s, and attained the cruising speed we always wanted at 15 knots.

"George McQueen of McQueen Boat Works in Vancouver built our 38-foot *Gibson Gal* and two others of a similar plan. Ours was number two off the line. George had a habit when 'lofting' the lines of the new vessel on the shipyard floor, to make minor modifications to 'sweeten up' the lines, the flare, the rake and tumblehome. Ed Monk liked the improvements so much, he ordered a 40-footer from McQueen, which he cruised in for many years." [18]

More than six of these round-bottom, semi-planing boats were built, with various engines, all capable of close to 20 knots. Monk's new boat from McQueen, *Tatoosh*, was launched in 1959, powered by a single 6-71 Detroit diesel. As with *Whim*, he installed an auxiliary motor for trolling and emergency power, a five hp diesel with V-drive and a retractable propeller shaft. An oil stove for heating and cooking meant that only one type of fuel was carried on board.

"Monk had followed the war changes in hard driving planing hulls, and knew that it was time to initiate a better planing hull for his types. The monohedron hull does not indicate a bottom shape peculiar to any one designer ... it is a theoretical characteristic of all planing hulls. Monk's designs were his own interpretation to give more speed, but with comfort in northwest waters and good horsepower efficiency. The beam-to-length ratio possible with this hull enabled him to design bigger and better interiors and use the beaminess for height configurations and fly bridge arrangements." *Pacific Motor Boat.* [55]

"It is only natural to desire a stout hull and with the custom-built boat the owner sometimes has conceptions of his own, particularly as to plank thickness, perhaps because this is the only thing between him and the water and he often insists on good stout ribs. These two items comprise about one-third the weight of the hull; increasing them materially may seriously affect the performance of the boat. Boatbuilders are a conscientious lot, in one respect perhaps too conscientious, many feel that if one inch is good an inch and a quarter will be better. This often has disastrous results." Ed Monk. [56]

McQueen Boat Works was founded by George McQueen who started out working for a construction company in his early 20s, manufacturing furniture for Victory ships. He joined a small firm which was producing 27-foot cruisers, then he and a partner set up a business which became Western Craft, in North Vancouver, B.C. Two years later he left, to establish his own yard.

Retired, in his mid-70s, George described those early days. "You couldn't get marine gears, or you couldn't buy a marine motor, as such, not for pleasure, so we had to build our own motors, get the blocks ... but we never had gears on 'em, we just used to put what you call a bobtail, you put a thrust bearing where your takeoff for your fan would be, and so when you started the motor, you were in gear, you were going, ready or not! It was really something; these things sold for $1,500 or $1,800, a 17-foot runabout. Well, you learn a lot and you learned fast, because they wanted more boats built ... it just got bigger and bigger. I really went out on my own about '52, I guess, when I started McQueen Boat Works. Never looked back, never had a time when we didn't have a boat in front of us. That's not to mean that we made money on every boat, because you had to go down to the yard, you had to keep the doors open, that's the key to any business ... keep the men working and leave the doors open, somebody's going to come in.

"We built parts for four or five boats at a time, that's when we started to get some money behind us, and then we would do the hulls, about 28-footers, we'd do part hulls and just pull them up to the ceiling, and we'd bring them down and finish them one at a time. We had about four men, and we could do one from that state in about six or seven weeks, produce a complete boat. There wasn't a lot of wiring in those days, just wiring up a motor, and you had your running lights, sometimes not even a bilge pump, just a hand pump, and one battery."

George recalled the first time he met Ed Monk. "We had a customer come to see us with a plan, and we were going to build it. We were lofting it, and so Ed Monk came up to see the loft. We had done a few things which we thought, you know, would enhance the looks of the boat, and he came up and he agreed. He said, 'Oh, I haven't got enough in it yet.' So he went back ...

and just redrew part of it, not much; it wasn't very much that we did, we just laid out the stem a little bit so that it made more flare. He redrew it and then he said, 'I'll have one of those.' "

That was the start of a relationship which would last through each of their careers and result in the "Monk-McQueen" yachts recognized all over the world. "The brokers coined that name from their advertising. They just put the words together, shortened up their ads." The 38-footers led to 40-footers, then to 46- and 48-footers — so many that George lost count. The next move was to 54 feet, then to 70 feet, carvel-construction hulls — planked out of Philippine mahogany with red cedar topsides, bent-oak frames and Douglas fir keels. "It was satisfying to me, working with wood. We ordered our wood ahead of time, and then we'd pick it out. In planking, they got to know what we wanted. Sometimes it got real thin and we'd have to go to a mill, to quarter cut a log or split a cedar log so you get edge grain." On a large semi-planing hull, George explained, wood had the advantage of strength combined with lighter weight. Though the yard later switched to building with fibreglass, they used traditional methods through the 1970s, producing yachts which remained in pristine condition for many years. [57]

"Ed Monk was the most practical guy you could run into. He would bend over backwards to satisfy people; he was a real gentleman. The only thing about Ed, if he paused, that was like saying, 'For crying out loud, don't do it.' You had to read him, and he wouldn't give you straight answers, but if he paused ... well, look out, don't do it. He would maybe let you do it, but you were on your own." George McQueen. [58]

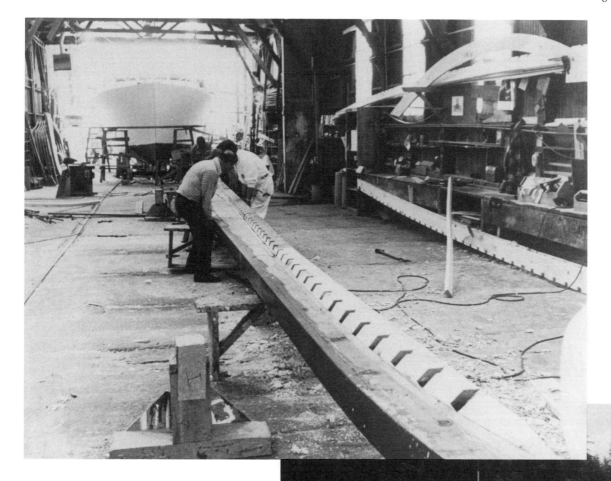

above: "Turning the keel" at McQueen Boat Works on the Fraser River, Vancouver, B.C. "McQueen boats weren't necessarily the length we set," recalled Ed Monk Jr. "If the keel timber was a little longer, they just didn't have the heart to cut it off, and they added a frame." [59] (PETER VASSILOPOULOS, COURTESY OF ED MONK JR.)

right: Tatoosh, *designed by Monk and "sweetened up" by George McQueen, later renamed* Lady Teodora, *owned by Wayne Smith of Victoria, B.C.* (COURTESY OF PAUL HELMAN)

Launching of La-Z-Buoy *at Esquimalt, B.C., August 1957. Plan No. 1758 (1952), extended from 32 to 34 feet by builder Warren Waterton. Graham and Jasmine Ross-Smith of Victoria, B.C., bought the boat from the Waterton family in 1991, and changed the name to* Aqualina. *The interior "has been updated to modern standards and taste without compromising its 'classic' qualities." Laid out with a typically efficient use of space: two single berths forward, main cabin dinette which folds down to a double berth, a tidy galley with an Olympic oil range, ice box, inside steering station, a comfortable settee with the back forming a hinged upper berth and storage below.* [60] (COURTESY OF GRAHAM ROSS-SMITH)

The more traditionally styled cruiser was still much in demand, travelling at eight knots instead of 14 or 15. The Forder Boat Company produced many 30- to 32-foot sedan cruisers; their 32-foot *Estralita*, with an aft cabin, was bought by Bob and Marci Plank of Kirkland, Washington, and renamed *Driftwood*. A flying bridge was added to *Driftwood* in 1995. The Allan Boat Works of Vancouver, B.C., launched *Mary Frances* in 1956 for Mary and Thomas Orr. She was renamed *Sonora*, and a command bridge was added by the second owner. The main cabin was over the engine, with two steps down to the galley, and a double-berth stateroom aft.

Dulwen was launched in 1957 at Philbrook's yard in Sidney, B.C., for Victoria residents Owen and Dulsie Fowler. Owen Fowler was the first commodore of the Capital City Yacht Club in Sidney, which was established in 1947 after starting out as a civil defence unit for patrolling local waters during World War II. *Dulwen* was later purchased by William Ovalle and Robert Peck of Vancouver, B.C.

In May 1958, Monk was nominated for the Puget Sound "Maritime Man Of The Year" award by the local Maritime Press Association. He had moved to new, larger premises at the National Building on the Seattle waterfront, and he hired several draftsmen, including Tom Van de Bogaart and Roy Wagner, who worked with him until the early 1960s. Newspapers and magazines reported a steady flow of launchings — from the 46-foot diesel harbour tug *Rufus*, built by Henry Long of Olympia, Washington, for Delta V. Smith, to *Anna Jackman* for Presbyterian missionary service in Juneau, Alaska.

The growing interest in sport fishing resulted in a variety of fast, V-bottom stock production designs — like the 28-foot "Ripple" sold by Forder. A safe boat for offshore trophy fishermen led to the development of the Grandy "Marlineer" series, ranging from 36 to 56 feet, marketed in California by businessman Ted Tate. While Monk was responsible for the original Marlineer hull, the stretched versions were drawn by Grandy foreman/loftsman Lynn Senour, who went on to set up his own successful design practice. Broad-beamed, with a sharp entrance, the Marlineers sliced through the waves at top speed. Grandy also built 40- to 48-footers for the sport fishing charter fleet at Westport, Washington. Light, inexpensive plywood boats for more sheltered waters — such as the 16-foot "Rivers Inlet," and the 26-foot "Swordfish" — came with paper templates for the hull framing and were "particularly suited to home construction." [19] The "Scat," a 14-foot runabout for water skiing and fishing, was "descended from a fairly long line of outboard boats which grew wider, faster, and improved in appearance with each new design." [20]

left: Sonora (ex-Mary Frances), *owned by Elmer and Luanna Buckingham of Burnaby, B.C. Forty feet long, with a 125 hp four cylinder Gray Marine Detroit engine. An ice box was installed under the cockpit seat, and a transom door led to a spacious swim grid — becoming standard by the late 1950s.* (COURTESY OF ELMER BUCKINGHAM)

below: Dulwen, *32 feet long, red cedar hull over oak ribs, Philippine mahogany house. The gas engine, a V-drive Chrysler V-8, was replaced in 1997 with a diesel.* Dulwen *has been used for year-round cruising by William Ovalle and Robert Peck of Vancouver, B.C.* (COURTESY OF ROBERT PECK)

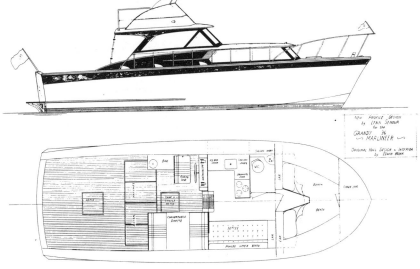

above: Sea trials on Puget Sound. Grandy Boat Company's 28-footer, which evolved from an earlier 27-foot design, dominated the local market in the late 1950s. (RAY KRANTZ, COURTESY OF FRED BAILEY)

right: Grandy "Marlineer," 36-foot offshore sport fishing cruiser, with new profile designed by Lynn Senour, original hull and interior drawn by Monk. "These were stunning boats." Fred Bailey, son of Grandy partner Henry Bailey. [61] (COURTESY OF FRED BAILEY)

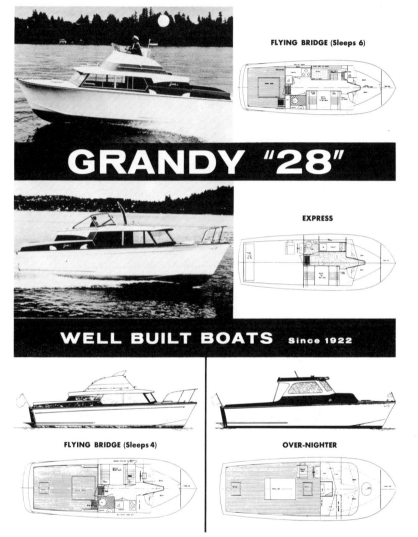

FLYING BRIDGE (Sleeps 6)

GRANDY "28"

EXPRESS

WELL BUILT BOATS Since 1922

FLYING BRIDGE (Sleeps 4)

OVER-NIGHTER

Grandy "28"

STANDARD EQUIPMENT: Four C. G. approved life preservers, electric horn, International navigation lights, marine toilet, upholstered foam rubber berths and dinette, fire extinguishers, bell, dock lines, lock lines, electric bilge blower, rubber muffler, alcohol plate, four rubber fenders with line, dish rack, ice chest, electric windshield wiper, electric bilge pump, mirror, medicine cabinet, pressure water system, chromed brass and polished stainless hardware.

OPTIONAL EQUIPMENT: Folding top, side curtains, cockpit cover, foam rubber driver and observer seats with foot rest, compass, Danforth anchor, anchor line and chain, anchor roller and deck plate, transom boarding platform, butane oven stove, cockpit steps, bow pulpit rail with flag staff, basin in head, aft cockpit seat to form berth, stainless handrails on side cabin.

28' MODELS

EXPRESS . .	4 Sleeper
SEDAN . . .	6 Sleeper
FLYING BRIDGE	4 Sleeper
FLYING BRIDGE	6 Sleeper
OVER-NIGHTER	2 Sleeper

Builder of the GRANDY 32', 36', 40', 44' and 48' cruisers, in various cabin and interior arrangements.

SPECIFICATIONS
For Listed Models

Length	28'
Beam	9' 10"
Draft	28"
Fuel Capacity	88 gal.
Water Capacity	40 gal.
Power Choice . .	177-210-225-260-280 hp. (single or twin)
Speed . . .	To 36 mph in light load condition

FAST   SEAWORTHY   DEPENDABLE

GENERAL SPECIFICATIONS: Hardwood stem, white-oak frames, transom and hull below waterline double planked. Planking above waterline red cedar. Fastened with Silicon bronze, brass and monel. Seams above waterline wedged and glued. Mahogany plywood deck fiberglass covered. Nautolex covering on cockpit floor. Cabin sides of solid mahogany. Ultrilite fiberglass sound proofing in engine room and cabin. Formica-covered table and drainboard. Linoleum in cabin. Side glass sliding in double, nylon-lined, stainless-steel track. Rudder, strut and shaft alley of manganese bronze. Monel shaft. Rubber stern bearing.

FOR'D AREA: Permanent vee double berth, storage beneath. Rope and chain locker. Streamlined deck hatch for ventilation and emergency exit.

MAIN CABIN: Upholstered foam rubber dinette (seats four comfortably) forming double berth. Formica covered table. Hanging locker. Ice box. Generous locker and storage space. Large drawers. Armstrong linoleum. Six sleeper has settee with hinged back forming upper and lower berth.

GALLEY: Stainless steel sink, dish rack, formica covered counter, ample storage, pressure water at faucet. Arranged for alcohol or butane stove.

HEAD: Separate room with full headroom. Manual marine toilet. Stainless wash-basin with pressure water at faucet. Formica counter. Locker space. Medicine cabinet, mirror.

COCKPIT AREA: Express model . . . . 11' length
Flying bridge model . . . 7' and 11' length
Over-nighter model . . . . 23' length

Grandy **BOAT COMPANY**

2538 Westlake North   Seattle 9, Washington

"WELL-BUILT BOATS" since 1922

Specification sheets for Grandy Boat Company "28." (COURTESY OF FRED BAILEY)

EDWIN MONK NAVAL ARCHITECT
26 FT. PLYWOOD   616 NAT'L. BLDG - SEATTLE 4, WN.
CRUISER DESIGN NO. 2172

THIS 26' CRUISER HAS A BEAM OF 9'-2" ~ IT IS A PLANING HULL WITH A TOP SPEED OF CLOSE TO 35 MILES WITH A 225 HP MOTOR AND IS WELL SUITED TO LESSER POWER AND LOWER SPEEDS. IT IS LEVEL RIDING AND BEING FAIRLY SHARP FORWARD, IS NOT A POUNDER. THE DINETTE FORMS A DOUBLE BERTH AND THERE ARE OVERNIGHT ACCOMODATIONS FOR FOUR.

PLANKING IS ⅜ PLYWOOD TOPSIDES AND ½ BOTTOM, THERE ARE 8 FRAMES AND IT IS A STURDY HULL WELL SUITED TO HOME CONSTRUCTION. THE PLANS ARE TO CONSIDERABLE DETAIL AND PAPER TEMPLATES OF THE ENTIRE HULL FRAMING ARE AVAILABLE. PLANS AND TEMPLATES ARE $135.00 AND PLANS ONLY ARE $75.00. BRONZE STRUT, RUDDER, ETC. ARE AVAILABLE FROM A LOCAL FIRM, FOR A REASONABLE FIGURE.

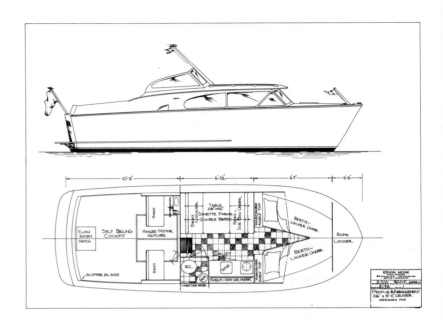

above: Plan No. 2172, 28-foot plywood cruiser by Forder Boatworks. "This was the real amateur's boat," said Ed Monk Jr. "Possibly the most popular stock design my father ever did. I'll bet that boat gave more fun, more enjoyment to people than any other boat." A 26-foot version, "Merrily," was tailored to the skills of the backyard builder and came with paper templates for the framing. Two berths in the forward stateroom, and two more on the convertible dinette. Galley with an oil or gas range, and an ice box under the forward dinette seat. 80 gallons of fuel, 30 gallons of water. Planing hull, capable of 20 knots. [62] (COURTESY OF ED MONK JR.)

right, top and bottom: Plan No. 2172. (COURTESY OF ED MONK JR.)

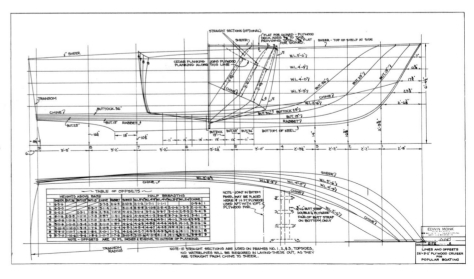

left: Fast yet seaworthy, with V-bottom, hard-chine hulls — vessels such as Tempest, for Gull Charters, were designed for the sport fishing trade from Westport, Washington, to San Diego, California. (RAY KRANTZ, COURTESY OF ED MONK JR.)

right: Coby (ex-Miramar, ex-Bridges), built by Tolly Tollefson in 1957, owned by Richard and Darlene Smith of Seattle. Length 60 ft., beam 14 ft., draft 4 ft. Twin Detroit 471 diesel engines. A true "showboat" with a glowing white hull, teak decks, varnished mahogany topsides, and gold-plated fittings, including the anchor and spotlight. (GREG GILBERT, COURTESY OF RICHARD AND DARLENE SMITH)

How To Buy A Boat: Liveaboards Susan MacDonald and John McOrmond of McMac Marine Services on northern Vancouver Island, restored their 40-foot sedan cruiser *Janra*, built by Ralph Maddison of Vancouver in the mid-1950s. It took the Maddison family 3,000 hours to complete *Janra*, in their backyard, and cost just under $6,000 for materials. The 225 hp Kermath engine was later replaced with a Chrysler 440, V-drive. The colour that the Maddisons chose for the hull and deck — turquoise — also showed up on *Whim* and many other 1950s boats. Susan MacDonald described the 1986 purchase of *Janra*: "Took possession on my fortieth birthday — I'm from the prairies and had barely been in a canoe before this. However, my boat partner (not John) was from the coast, although he had never had a 40-footer before. We had been looking at sailboats but couldn't find anything big enough at the price we could afford. Basically, we foolishly fell in love with her as we walked down the dock. When I did have her up for sale — in more than a year, I had one not-good-enough offer — I kept telling myself we couldn't have been the only fools in the world and someone else would eventually walk down that dock and have the same reaction we had. The irony is that both my boat partner and I did each end up moving on to her a second time. (Individually — he jumped ship and I stayed for a couple of years, then I moved off and he came back on. Eventually we switched again which was when John and I took her over for good and all.) So another fool — or fools — did walk down the dock, but it was the same fools." [63]

In addition to running his stock production company, Tolly Tollefson built a 56-foot cruiser which he sold to E. Anderson of Tacoma, Washington. Named *Bridges*, it was sold for salvage after a fire, and later rebuilt, and used for charters based out of Oak Harbor, Washington. Anderson commissioned a second *Bridges* from Tollefson, from the same plans as the first, lengthened four feet to accommodate twin GM diesels. The boat changed hands several times after Anderson died, and was renamed *Coby*, owned by Richard and Darlene Smith of Seattle, Washington.

Santa Barbara Yachts in southern California specialized in strip-planked versions of Monk's designs, "which makes for a very strong hull, with planking edge nailed and edge glued." [21] *Carowil* was one of several 38-footers launched at Santa Barbara, with trim, tri-cabin lines and a top speed of ten knots. The sturdy, 44-foot *Halcyon*, commissioned by Lee Gillette for use in southern waters, featured a large, open cockpit and flying bridge. By the end of the 1950s the "heavy-duty cruiser" was coming into its own, with yards from Australia to Florida receiving orders for similar designs.

Monk-designed cutter Bendora *giving* Trekka *a tow into Oak Bay, near Victoria, B.C., at the termination of Guzzwell's epic circumnavigation.* (COURTESY OF GORDON NICKELLS)

Seattle boatbuilder John Guzzwell's first project was the 21-foot *Trekka*, which he sailed solo around the world, setting off from Victoria, B.C., in 1955 and returning in 1959. He then offered to help a friend, Paul Whittier, who wanted to build a fast power boat in the style of the late 1920s. "Paul commissioned Mr. Monk to draw up a 64-foot motor yacht that was twin screw and had a canoe stern. This boat was built almost entirely out of Douglas fir marine plywood which was used for not only the planking but for interior partitions, bulkheads, deckworks, you name it, it was built out of plywood." Paul Whittier had set out to prove that plywood was a viable material for boat construction, which is why he enlisted the services of a top designer, and brought up a builder from southern California who was very experienced in plywood construction. "Soon after I joined the project in the spring of 1960, Paul decided to add another four feet to the mid section making the boat 67 feet overall. I don't think Ed Monk was particularly happy at his new design being altered at such an early stage but we used to see him come to view the construction and I guess he accepted what was going on without getting too upset!

"The boat was built upside down and we turned it over fairly easily using overhead chain lifts. Before it was complete, I left to go to England to build my own boat, *Treasure*, which I still have." In 1972 John sailed *Treasure* from Hawaii to Alaska, then down the Inside Passage, stopping to visit Paul Whittier, "to see the vessel I had worked on and which had provided me with much useful information in using glue laminated construction." The boat had been called *Paollape*, from a collection of Whittier family names. It was later sold and renamed *Snobird*; in 1994 John had the opportunity to go aboard, and check out his early work. [64]

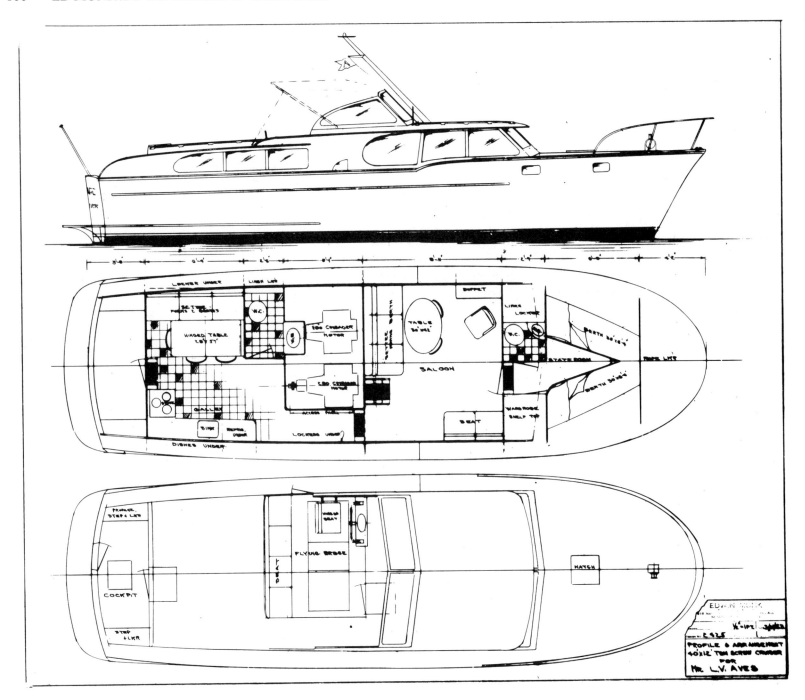

Plan No. 2425, 40-foot twin-screw cruiser for L. Aves, Vancouver,
B.C. (COURTESY OF ED MONK JR.)

CHAPTER SIX

PROGRESS ... IN STYLE

THE 1960S BROUGHT growth and prosperity to all aspects of the maritime economy — from commercial shipping to resource-based industries like logging and fishing, to boating for recreation. The expectations of the "average" boaters were rising, along with their disposable income. In addition to Garden, Hanson, and Monk, designers such as Ben Seaborn and Arthur DeFever were making names for themselves along the west coast.

The job of the naval architect "is to put into functional and pleasing form the practical — and perhaps a few of the impractical — ideas of the owner," Monk wrote in 1963. "Don't hesitate to present your ideas and don't abandon them without good reason. Many ideas that seem at first without merit have, on a little more consideration and perhaps with slight changes, resulted in decided improvement or advance." [1] Customers have a lot more to do with design than the architect, he added. "Women have brought about a lot of improvements by insisting on space, light, airiness, open areas which take the best advantage of the best weather. Above all they demand stability and safety while their husbands continue to look out for peak performance." [2]

Monk's approach to his work had been largely influenced by the distinguished naval architect Norman L. Skene, author of *Elements Of Yacht Design*. In his book, Skene laid out the three goals for a boat — performance, comfort, and appearance. At least one of these goals would be sacrificed for the others, which is what Monk emphasized with his clients: "A boat is truly a compromise and this holds true even when weight and beauty and smartness are considered." [3]

Developing a plan meant taking a client through every decision — from the shape of the hull to the final colour choice. Hull shape — which has the most effect on performance — was not always a priority with his

"The designer welcomes all the information his client can bring him, including clippings and photos. A sketch, no matter how crude, is a real help. Generally the sketcher forgets that a hull has flare and that the floor line is much narrower than the deck line, and that he is actually drawing berths, toilets, basins, etc, on the outside of the hull if they are in the bow ...." Ed Monk. [65]

"The question of what form makes for the best and most comfortable sea boat is of paramount importance. The shape of the bow largely dictates whether a hull will give her passengers a comparatively smooth ride or a rough one; whether she will be a dry or wet boat; and it has a great influence on efficiency under power. However, there seems to be no agreement among naval architects. Each works into his designs whatever shape his experience seems to dictate." Ed Monk. [66]

"In medium-speed boats particularly, the difference between hard-chine and round-bilge hulls can be merely one of aesthetics .... The round-bilge version will be a bit easier riding but will have a tendency to roll a bit more deeply, while the hard-chine version will feel steadier but have a slightly snappier roll. Nevertheless, as a general rule, hard chines are for high-speed inshore work and round bilges are for low-speed offshore work." Dave Gerr. [67]

"I drove a Model T Ford in 1928 from Winnipeg to Vancouver, and got a job in a garage near Chinatown. It was from seven at night to eight in the morning, 13 hours, seven days a week. Then I got a job at a garage at 13th and Granville, the shift was a bit better, from five to two in the morning. My brother came out a year and a half later, and we got a job at Vancouver Shipyard as apprentices at five cents an hour. We were living in Kitsilano, in the top part of a big house, and there was a garage out back. We got the idea of building a speedboat. We built a 21-footer, with an old car engine in it, and it did pretty good. We eventually sold that, and I gave up boating until the 1950s, when I got my first Monk.

"I met Ed Monk in the late 1940s, around 1949. I went down to Seattle and went out to the island where he lived, and he took me for a ride on his boat. He built a very simple boat — he didn't panel all the inside, you could see the ribs, and that way it went faster, but it was a really well-built boat. There weren't many people around at that time who were designing good-looking boats. When I went to see him, I had a lot of confidence in him. He was a very simple man, but a real gentleman. You always felt comfortable doing business with him. I had a lot of dealings with him over the years, a lot of phone calls and trips to see him. He built his boats light and strong ... he was very good at balancing a boat." Robert Osborne, founder of Osborne Propellers, North Vancouver, B.C. [68]

customers, Monk noted. Their two most common questions were "How many will she sleep?" and "How fast does she go?" [4] A hard chine hull was fast and light, so that it could lift partly out of the water, or plane. A semi-planing, round-bottom hull — with its bilge sharply rounded and underbody kept fairly flat — combined the virtues of the V bottom and the round bottom but again needed to be light. The full round-bottom hull — such as on a deep-water, trawler-style pleasure boat — was strong and seaworthy, but slow.

Twin engines gave more security and maneuverability, but with added weight and cost, and unprotected propellers, an important factor in the northwest. "There is a fallacy that twin engines will produce a faster boat than a single of the same total horsepower, and another that diesel horsepower is somehow more powerful than gasoline horsepower. The latter misconception is probably based on the fact that diesel can be operated continuously closer to its top RPM." [5] As for the final look: "The architect can furnish the owner with several black-or-blue-line prints with a white background, then, with a box of color pencils ... the owner or his wife can try their hands at finding pleasing color schemes — pleasing at least to those to whom it really matters." [6]

One of Monk's more experienced customers was Robert Osborne, who started out in the early 1950s with the 30-foot *Brenhines Y Mor*, Welsh for Queen of the Sea, constructed by his brother, Bill Osborne, in Port Alberni, B.C., and brought to Vancouver on a flatcar. The 48-foot *Brenhines II*, launched in 1959, was the first Monk design built by A.C. Benson Shipyards in Vancouver, a Coal Harbour company founded in 1919 with a long history of wood-vessel construction and repair. By the early 1960s, according to Robert Benson, the demand for wood vessels was minimal, and the yard gradually switched to aluminum and steel.

In 1961 the Benson shipyard company was contracted to build four 47-foot bridge-deck cruisers, one of which would be *Brenhines III*. "What happened," explained Robert Osborne, "is that no sooner did I get my boat built, than somebody wanted to buy it." The others were *Dorlen* for Len Sewell, *Lady Diane* for Harold Elworthy of Island Tug and Barge, and *Breezin Thru* for Jack McDonald of Burrard Shipyard. The round-bottom hulls had one-inch yellow cedar planking below the waterline, red cedar above; decks were teak, and cabins mahogany. "These were all fantastic boats. Round chine, instead of a hard chine. With round chine, the ribs are bent around and it makes a good sea boat. If you had seas coming at you from the side, they would kind of roll with it. Hard chine — we put a corner on it. Made them go faster." [7]

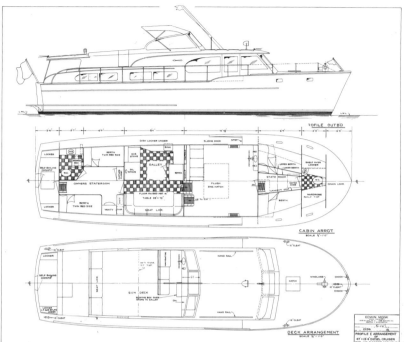

above: Escalante *(ex-Dorlen), Vancouver Wooden Boat Festival winner. Cruising speed of 10½ knots with a single GM 8 V-71 NA. "A very soft-riding vessel, she handles extremely well — even better with the addition of a bowthruster." L. H. "Mike" Michalson of Vancouver, B.C., who, with his wife, Joan, bought* Escalante *in 1971 from Len Sewell.* (69) *Another boat show prizewinner,* Lady Diane, *was owned by Irving Dowman of Victoria, B.C.* (COURTESY OF L.H. MICHALSON)

right: Robert Osborne's 47-foot bridge-deck cruiser. (COURTESY OF ED MONK JR.)

below: Four sister ships on sea trials in Vancouver Harbour, 1961: Lady Diane, Dorlen *(later* Escalante)*,* Breezin Thru *(later* Sequoia Park*) and* Brenhines III *(later* Keo Keo)*.* (COURTESY OF L.H. MICHALSON)

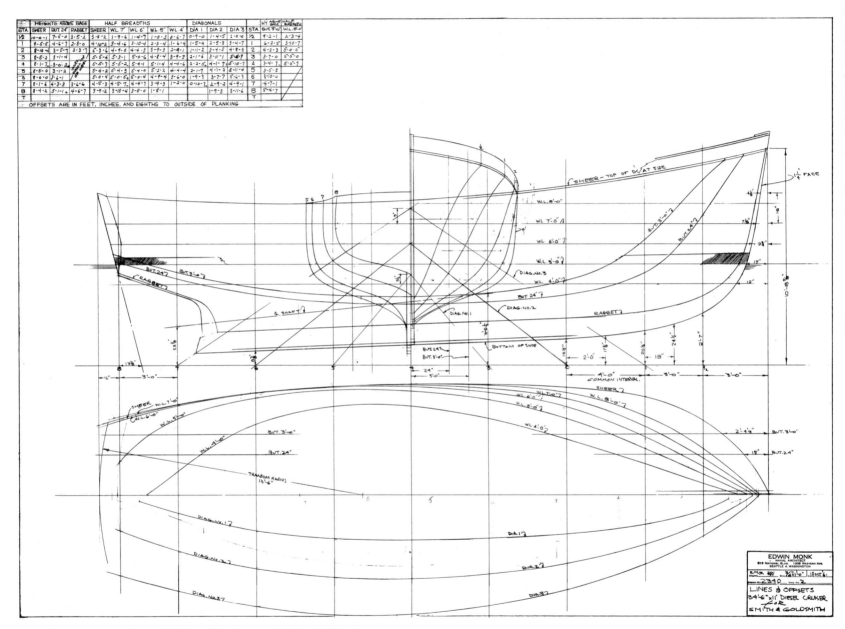

Plan No. 2340, lines and offsets of diesel cruiser Goldsmith Maid,
length 34½ ft., beam 11 ft. (COURTESY OF ED MONK JR.)

Ed Monk and his wife Ann had a son, Robert Edwin, and a daughter, Judy (later Judy Wade). Robert Edwin, known as Ed Monk Jr., worked part-time with his father, graduating from the University of Washington with a degree in industrial design. "When I was a late teenager," he recalled, "my father said, 'I've got to do a boat design for the Douglas Fir Plywood Association.' Grandy's had built one, to prove the plan worked. They used to sell the plans for two bits or a dollar a copy. My father said, 'Let's see if a real amateur can build one. If you'll build one, I'll give you all the materials.' Of course I took the bait and ran, and put a lot of miles on that boat." He built several more runabouts, designing them himself. "These were fast things ... great big engines, they were noisy and broke down, but I taught more people to water ski." [8] He gained experience working at the Grandy yard and with Bud Forder, for whom he developed much affection and respect. After returning to college to study engineering, he was certified as a naval architect. He joined his father's practice full-time in 1963, beginning with the job of working on deep-V-hulled power boats, which had been pioneered by Ray Hunt.

"Mother is probably the only woman who spent her life living in a house that never had one room completely finished. Closet doors were never put on the closets upstairs, molding was missing in most rooms, etc. etc. BUT ... every single boat had all her gear, cupboard doors and finishing touches. We all knew where his heart was!" Judy (Monk) Wade. [70]

Ed and Ann Monk with their children, Judy and Ed Jr., with one of Monk's famous "build-your-own" dinghies in the background. (COURTESY OF JUDY WADE)

RESIDENCE PHONE BAINBRIDGE ISLAND VIKING 2-4256   OFFICE PHONE MUTUAL 2-4317

Edwin

Monk

NAVAL ARCHITECT

616 National Building   Seattle 4, Washington

Mr. J. Dryburgh   Feb. 9, 1962
6431 Patricia Bay Hwy.
Royal Oak, B.C.

Dear Mr. Dryburgh:

Am enclosing a descriptive sheet on our 15'2" plywood
outboard that would seem suitable for your purpose.
This pretty well outlines its construction and gives
an idea of materials required.

They are good little boats, quite ruggedly constructed
and not too difficult to build. The approximate weight
of the boat is 300 pounds; transom width is 4'9".

Included in the plans are prints showing it as a runabout as well as with shelter cabin, building instructions, fastening list and lumber order.

                                Sincerely,

                                EDWIN MONK

EM:ab
encl

PLEASURE AND COMMERCIAL CRAFT   WOOD AND STEEL

Thirty-foot tugboat J & D *commissioned in 1960 by J. Williams, who had a contract for cleaning logging debris in the Alberni Canal. Fir planking, gumwood sheathing, gumwood stem. Built by Jim Dryburgh of D & L Boatworks on the Saanich Peninsula, near Victoria, B.C. Jim Dryburgh apprenticed at a yard on Wharf Street in Victoria, helping to build* Hi-Seas *and many other Monk designs. In 1964 he moved his shop to Oak Bay, where he operated Oak Bay Boatworks for 30 years.* (COURTESY OF JIM DRYBURGH)

(COURTESY OF JIM DRYBURGH)

Ann Monk was a lifelong cruising companion for her husband, and the family could be found out boating year round, often visiting their waterfront cottage in Ganges on Saltspring Island, B.C. In 1964 they set off in *Tatoosh* to circumnavigate Vancouver Island, "this continent's greatest and most varied cruising coastline, one of the most distinctive in the world." They were accompanied by two other boats, Bob Taylor and his family on the 83-foot *Elfin*, and Bill Paine and his family on the 53-foot *Una Mae*. "The Canadians have turned out some splendid large scale charts ... and the B.C. Pilot is a great help," noted Monk. "A radar would be wonderful, but most of us have to be satisfied with more modest equipment, such as a good depthsounder and a good compass." Rounding the northern tip of the island, they barely saw Cape Scott through the rain and the murk. They were glad to take on a mooring buoy in Sea Otter Cove, "where four trollers waited out the weather, one with a deer hanging in the rigging." They watched whales being brought into the whaling station at Coal Harbour, and sampled a piece, deciding that it tasted similar to beef. They explored the inlets southward, stopping at Friendly Cove and then Hot Springs — for a "much-needed bath." [9] It was a pleasurable trip, even more so because of *Tatoosh*'s diesel engine, the first diesel that Monk had used. "When you step on the starter, you don't wonder if you have gas in the bilges. Diesels are reliable. They always seem to start, and if one can afford diesel power, we highly recommend it." [10]

Rob Roy, a 41½-foot tri-cabin cruiser owned by Bob and Margaret Cross of Victoria, was built by Ernest Phillips of Vancouver for Archie Gardiner in 1965. The centre bridge, originally under canvas, was permanently enclosed, a renovation seen on many bridge-deck cruisers. With twin Ford 390 gas engines, 240 hp each, *Rob Roy* had a top speed of 20 knots, a planing speed of 14 knots, and a cruising speed of nine knots.

Plans for one of Monk's motor sailers were published in *Pacific Yachting* magazine and caught the eye of Rod Knight of Sooke, B.C. Rod contracted Phil and Doug Barron to build him a hull, carvel-planked fir on oak frames, and in 1965 the 46-foot ketch *Manathine* was launched at the Barrons' East Sooke yard. Rod completed *Manathine* himself, describing her as safe and stable; she crossed to Hawaii three times and in the mid-1970s the Knight family made a 32-month cruise around the South Pacific. *Manathine* had a round bottom and full keel with a cutaway forefoot, and carried 8,000 pounds of ballast. The large centre cockpit had a covered steering station and was finished nicely in weathered teak; the hull and topsides were painted white. Down below, the cosy aft cabin

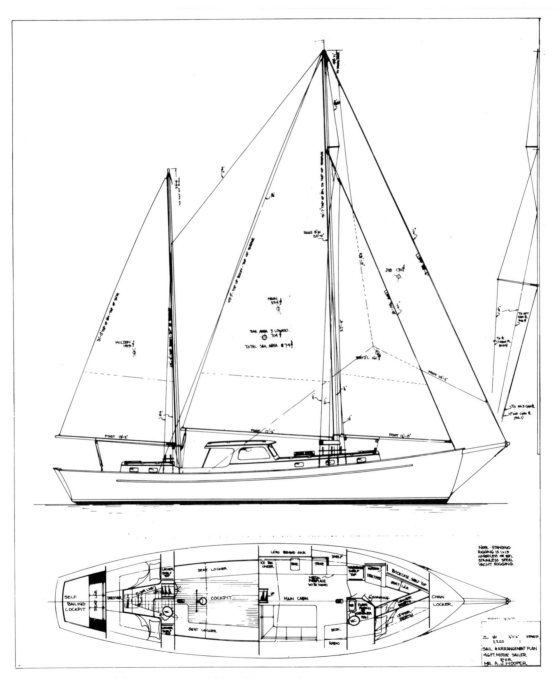

Plan No. 2220, 46-foot motor sailer Mikay IV, *sister ship to*
Manathine. (COURTESY OF ED MONK JR.)

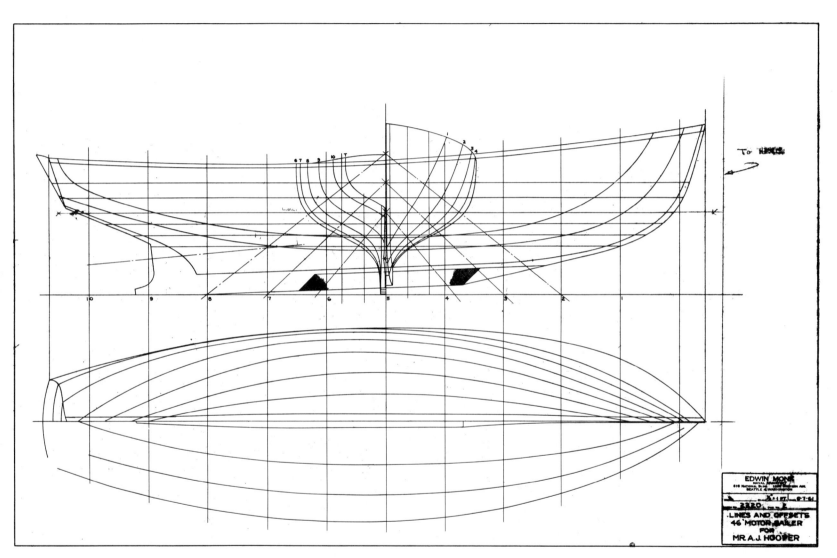

Plan No. 2220, lines and offsets of motor sailer. (Courtesy of Ed Monk Jr.)

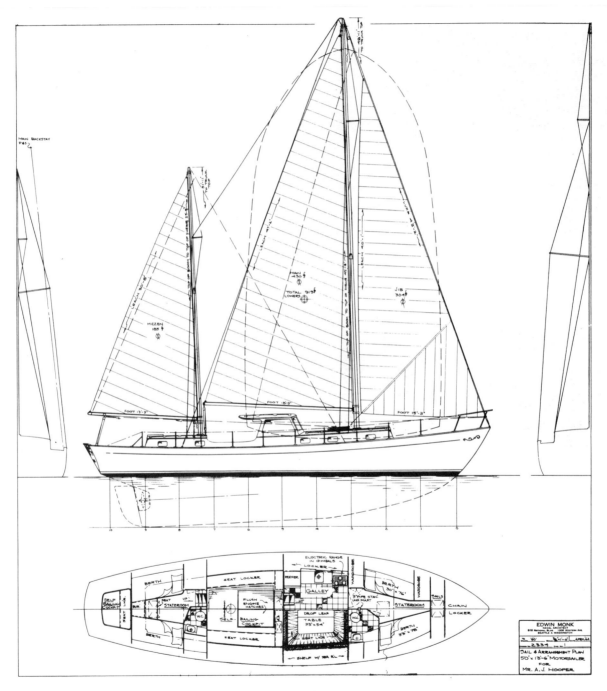

Moonraker, Plan No. 2334, 50-foot motor sailer for J. Hooper, built by Santa Barbara Yachts, California. (COURTESY OF ED MONK JR.)

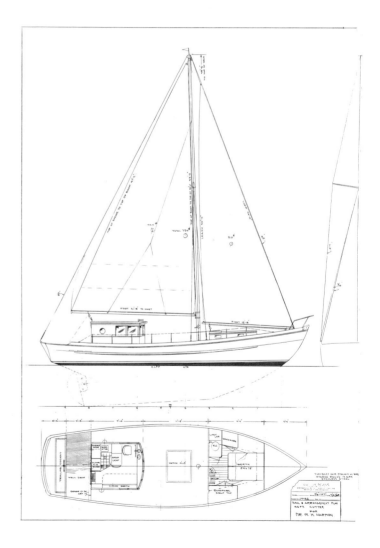

above: Moonraker *off Santa Catalina Island, California. Described by Ed Monk Jr. as "a handsome boat, and famous in its own right,"* Moonraker *gave rise to the fibreglass "Searaker 50," cutter or ketch rig, offered by Windward Marine of Tacoma, Washington.* [71] (SANTA BARBARA YACHTS, COURTESY OF ED MONK JR.)

right: Plan No. 1096, 42-foot schooner outfitted as a fishing vessel for R.H. Harmon. The lines of the schooner gave rise to a number of later designs, including the "Tradewind 47," and the "Skookum" hulls designed by Ed Monk Jr. (COURTESY OF ED MONK JR.)

contained a head and bunks, the galley and settees were in the main cabin, and forward was a ¾ berth. *Manathine* was kept in the family for more than 30 years, later owned by Rod's son, Michael Knight, of Sidney, B.C.

A sister ship, *Mikay IV*, was built for J. Hooper by Santa Barbara Yachts. The centre cockpit was well suited to warm weather and provided complete privacy for the owner and guests, with staterooms at each end of the hull. The owner commissioned Monk to design him a second motor sailer, the 50-foot ketch *Moonraker*, more spacious but similarly arranged.

Many of Monk's new customers were looking for a "heavy duty" cruiser, the design that had evolved from the west-coast troller, "almost the ultimate in the small sea-going boat." [11] Designing a boat for the open ocean presented problems, not the least being roll. One solution that Monk experimented with was a steadying sail, which required that the boat carry ballast. Bilge keels were useful on larger vessels, but only when the vessel was under way. "Doubtless the most effective device is the fin type, usually hydraulically actuated, and controlled by a gyro," he concluded. [12] The hydraulic-activated fins were also expensive, and many pleasure boats adopted a version of the fishermen's stabilizers or "flopper-stoppers," which proved very effective at anchor and at speeds of less than ten knots.

Scaup, with bridge added, and stabilizing poles based on the "flopper-stoppers" used by west-coast fishermen. (DAVID CARERE, COURTESY OF JOHN WEST)

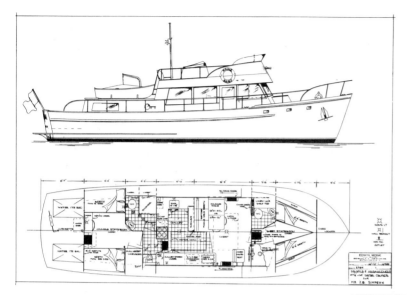

above: Heavy-duty cruiser Coya, Plan No. 2384, for J. Simpson of Vancouver, B.C. (COURTESY OF ED MONK JR.)

above right: Coya, looking aft, with galley to starboard. (G. SIMPSON, COURTESY OF JIM GENGE)

right: Coya, length 47 ft., beam 14 ft., draft 5 ft., displacement 44,000 pounds, 180 hp Caterpillar engine. Round-bottom hull planked with red cedar above the waterline, fir below, gumwood keel, mahogany joinery inside. (G. SIMPSON, COURTESY OF JIM GENGE)

Wood Duck (ex-*Patti Marie*), length 42 ft., beam 13 ft. 4 in., draft 4 ft. Powered by a GM 6-71 diesel with a dry stack exhaust. A sister ship was built for E.L. Whitebone at West Bay Boat Builders (later West Bay SonShip Yachts) in Delta, B.C. *Wood Duck*'s funnel, a distinctive Monk feature, housed the chimneys for the engine exhaust and the oil stove or furnace, in addition to providing convenient storage topsides. Typical of the tri-cabin design, *Wood Duck* was laid out comfortably for a family or guests: double bunks forward, a convertible couch in the main cabin, and a deluxe master stateroom, with a built-in desk and a bathtub in the head. "She handles very well and will go straight astern in reverse. The walk-around decks and raised bulwarks are great. Originally, she was not well finished inside and needed much attention. The galley was extended, a dinette was put in, along with a general renewal of cosmetics. A few years later, I gutted the aft cabin and changed it to the present design. We've added a lot of new equipment over the years." Ian Kenning. [72] (Bruce Kenning, courtesy of Ian Kenning)

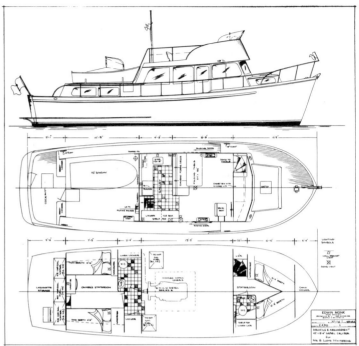

above: Plan 2450, sister ship to Wood Duck. (COURTESY OF ED MONK JR.)

left: Wood Duck (BRUCE KENNING, COURTESY OF IAN KENNING)

Stately and solid, the 47-foot *Coya* was launched at Philbrook's yard in Sidney for J. Simpson of Vancouver, B.C., in 1963. *Coya* was purchased several years later by Jim Genge of Sidney, and was used for numerous voyages to Alaska. Like *Coya*'s designer, Jim Genge believed that a boat should be simple, functional and practical. *Coya* was kept outside, with naturally weathered teak decks, swim grid and hand railings; the cap rails and rub rails were painted gray. The engine room had a built-in work bench, and on the bow was a commercial type windlass for the 100-pound CQR anchor. Large windows made for a bright main cabin; the galley had a Pacific Dickinson stove and full-size double sink. The 180 hp Caterpillar used four gallons of fuel per hour at 1,550 rpm, giving a speed of eight knots.

Similar vessels were being launched at the McQueen Boat Works, including the 46-foot *Branta II*, commissioned by Monty Porter, later purchased by Mike and Barbara Stone of Maple Bay, B.C. *Branta II* was outfitted with a bowthruster, hot-water heating, and a G71-N GM diesel with a range of 1,000 miles at nine knots.

Patti Marie, Plan No. 2469, was built at Craine Boat Works of Everett, Washington, for Mr. and Mrs. J. Sponek in 1965. Ian and Margaret Kenning of Victoria, B.C., bought *Patti Marie* in 1983, renaming her *Wood Duck*. Decks were fibreglass over plywood, and the round-bottom hull was yellow cedar below the waterline, red cedar above, 1³/₈ inch planking on 1⁷/₁₆ inch by two-inch bent-oak frames. Jack Craine also built the 50-foot displacement cruiser *Lady S*, for his own use.

Two 52-footers built to the same hull plan in the mid-1960s were *Mardick*, at Withey Shipyard on Gabriola Island, B.C., and *Cebu*, at Ponce Shipyard in the Philippines. *Mardick*, for Seattle owner Richard Jones, was outfitted with a single D-333 Caterpillar engine and carried 750 gallons of fuel, with a range of 1,200 miles. The steel-hulled *Cebu* had two six cylinder Ford diesels and carried 2,100 gallons of fuel, with a range of 2,400 miles. Monk considered steel better suited for a large, offshore vessel, since it was easier to repair and the tanks could be built in, eliminating wasted space around metal tanks in a wood boat. Steel was considerably heavier, though, and *Cebu*'s ³/₁₆ inch thick hull, which met Lloyd's standards, weighed twice as much as *Mardick*'s hull, planked with 1 ³/₈ inch cedar. In addition, *Cebu*'s living quarters required insulation against heat and cold.

Altogether different vessels built of steel were the 48-foot *Sword Fish*, designed for the waters off San Francisco — with nine swivel seats in the cockpit, high freeboard and generous flare — and the 65-foot stern-

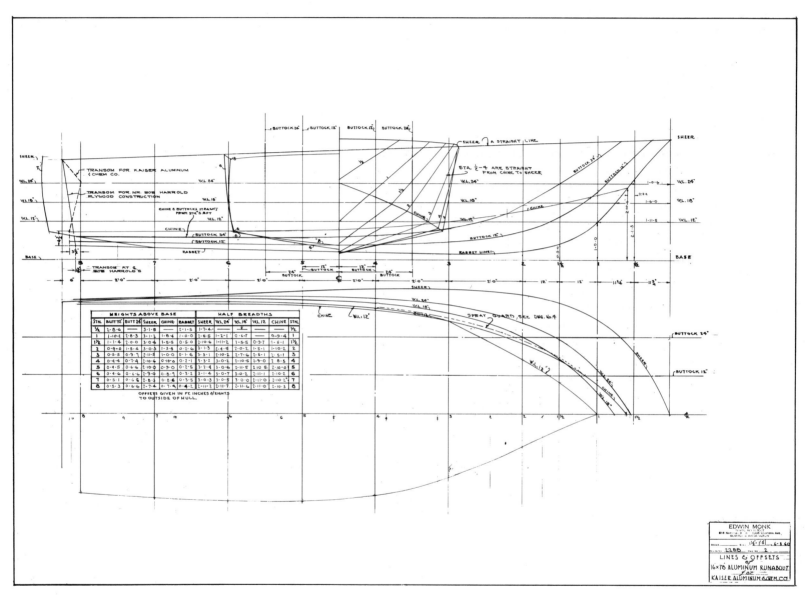

*Plan No. 2288, lines and offsets of aluminum runabout, length 16
ft., beam 78 in., for Kaiser Aluminum & Chemical Company.
(COURTESY OF ED MONK JR.)*

wheeler *River Queen*, a "dine and dance" boat for Portland, Oregon. John Nardone built the 38-foot steel V-bottom cruiser *Jeana S* for his own use. A growing number of clients were requesting aluminum hulls, "the problem here is that the material is costly, but there is a big advantage in the light weight of the material." [13] Carter Machine Works in New Westminster, B.C., built *Silver Lady*, a 45-foot, aluminum V-bottom cruiser for company owner L.A. Carter, and Benson shipyards built the 60-foot *Abashag*, another V-bottom planing hull, twin screw with right angle drives, for Lee Dunavent of Seattle.

Consistent with his belief that boatbuilding could be inexpensive, Monk drew a few designs which could be constructed out of ferrocement. It was a material he considered best suited to heavy commercial use, noting that "ferrocement boats seem to run heavier in total weight than anticipated." By far the strongest trend was to fibreglass, in both factory and custom production, "and its use no doubt will increase as time goes on due to its numerous advantages." [14]

Peter Bracken's shipyard near Sydney, Australia, completed orders for the 46-foot *Antipodes* and several other yachts and police boats, and the Dutch-based De Vries Lentsch yard built a 68-foot pleasure cruiser for Mr. Sugarman. Although these and other commissions — for small ferry boats, search and rescue boats, and simple plywood runabouts — filled the drawing boards, there was still time to think about a new boat for the Monk family, replacing the 40-foot *Tatoosh*. In 1965 *Nika Sia* was launched at McQueen Boat Works, Monk's first pilothouse yacht, 46 feet overall, with a six cylinder Cummins diesel giving a speed of 12 knots. Planking was Alaska yellow cedar below the waterline, red cedar above, on oak frames — Monk's preference for all of his boats. He wanted an easy care, "sociable" boat, with a painted superstructure and exterior brightwork kept to a minimum. The mahogany-panelled main cabin was open and uncluttered with an L-shaped settee which converted to a bed; the coffee table rose to the height of a dining table, and chairs could be arranged as needed. Both sleeping cabins were in the bow: "the skipper should sleep in the forward stateroom even though it may not be the most comfortable," to monitor the anchor. [15]

The pilothouse layout combined the qualities of a modern ocean cruiser with a lighter, faster hull for inside waters. "The high bow should be a decided advantage in a head sea, making for a drier and safer boat. The most comfortable navigating position under these conditions is aft, rather than forward. As Tolly Tollefson remarked, the most comfortable position would be right over the transom. Visibility, however, forces a compromise."

right: Island Trader, *90-foot freight boat for* Ketchikan Transportation Company. (RAY KRANTZ, COURTESY OF ED MONK JR.)

below: Jimax III, *68-foot, steel-hulled, built by* G. de Vries Lentsch, Amsterdam. (COURTESY OF ED MONK JR.)

The pilothouse was placed as far aft as possible, with the flying bridge above taking up the entire width across. *Nika Sia*'s beam was 14½ feet, which "for a 46-foot boat may seem excessive, but in this case the width at the waterline is only a little more than normal and the hull flares out almost all the way aft, tumbling home slightly at the transom. This adds very little to the cost of building. The wider side deck obtained, in this instance 17 inches, is to me decidedly worthwhile." The round-bottom monohedron hull made for a level ride, and "a reverse to the frame heels next to the keel adds to the draft ... an asset in a sea boat." [16] A sister ship was built by Keeler Boats of Portland, Oregon, one of dozens of successful variations on *Nika Sia*'s lines.

Vancouver businessman Bob Gibson's second *Gibson Gal* was a pilothouse cruiser, also built by McQueen. The 51-foot *Sea Lure II* came from the Withey yard on Gabriola Island, another pilothouse layout with a single D-333 Caterpillar engine. *Cee-Aer*, the largest pleasure boat ever built at the Withey yard, was launched in 1968 for Vancouver broker Robert Hall. The 65-foot *Cee-Aer* had two 300 hp Cummins diesels and a rosewood-panelled interior, and took ten men 15 months to complete.

"The addition of one or two small items of equipment will not have any great effect, but it is the cumulative effect of a large number of small things that does the damage. Every man who has sold his boat and removed his personal belongings has marveled at the number of times he filled the car in packing them home. I have to keep a close watch on the first mate as her ambition seems to be to transfer as many cases of canned goods from the grocery store to the boat as is possible." Ed Monk. [73]

"Choosing a name should be the easiest part in building a new boat but somehow this is not always the case. Indian names both euphonious and with appropriate meaning seem difficult to find. The name chosen for this particular boat was *Nika Sia* which means 'My Love' in the Chinook jargon." Ed Monk. [74]

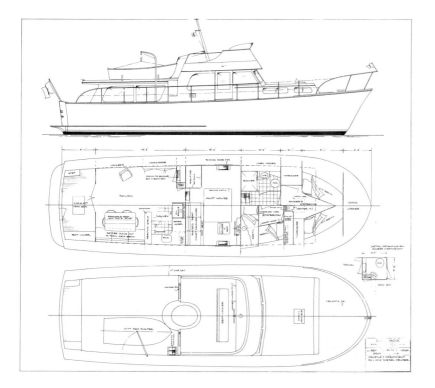

left: Nika Sia, *46-foot pilothouse cruiser, Plan No. 2507. "When the naval architect designs a new boat for his personal use as well as for others, the exposure of this plan to readers takes on special significance. The reader can see what this designer thinks can be done, what he personally prefers and perhaps what compromises he has carried on with the kind of cruising his family shares with him." Ed Monk.* [75]

left: Ceara II *(ex-Gibson Gal, ex-Decibelle), length 51 ft., beam 14 ft. 8 in., draft 4 ft. 4 in. Owned by Jim Brass and Susan Usher, Comox B.C. Two staterooms forward, pilothouse with twin Detroit 6V53 diesel engines below, large cabin aft with galley and dinette.* (COURTESY OF JIM BRASS)

below: Sea Lure II, *length 51 ft., beam 15 ft., draft 5 ft. Hard-chine hull, built by Withey Shipyard on Gabriola Island, B.C. Owned by Gordon and Darlene Weir of Comox, B.C.,* Sea Lure II *has cruised from the Columbia River to Alaska.* (COURTESY OF GORDON AND DARLENE WEIR)

The 40-foot express cruiser *Mar Lo* was built by Lloyd Griffith at Franklin River, on Vancouver Island, B.C., in the late 1960s, and later renamed *Chris Mar*, owned by Dougall and Erma Warren of Ladysmith, B.C. Lloyd Griffith had built several other Monk designs during the 1950s, including the 38-foot bridge-deck cruiser *Playboy*.

In 1967 the Seventh Day Adventist Church contracted Monk to design a boat to be used for mission work on the central B.C. coast. The 49-foot *Northern Light* came from Matsumoto Shipyard in North Vancouver, one of the first yards to use aluminum, which formed the deckhead and cabin sides. *Northern Light* was sold in 1976 to Roy Hales, who cruised to Alaska many times. Arthur and Heather Rendell of Vancouver, B.C., purchased the boat in 1995.

Bill Osborne began construction on a new boat for his brother Robert in Vancouver, B.C., completing the 54-foot *Rao* in 1968. At least six others were built to *Rao*'s design, which featured a bent-frame, V-bottom hull, "a strong and fairly light method of framing a V-bottom in which the chine is superimposed over the frames and disappears forward, giving the appearance of a round bottom hull." [17] A few years later Robert added eight feet to the stern, giving more cockpit space. *Rao*'s engine room below the main cabin was well-planned and immaculate, as one would expect from an owner who understood machinery from the inside out. The twin V-12s were replaced with eight cylinder V92 TAs, with an increase in running speed from 17 knots to 20 knots. *Rao* was fast, without sacrificing strength: the bottom was planked with 1½ inch mahogany below the waterline, 1⅓ inch red cedar above, and the superstructure was solid Honduras mahogany. A couch and easy chairs filled the main cabin; across from the steering station was a good-sized bench seat, the back of which formed a bar. Several steps led to the galley and upholstered dinette, on a lower level, refurbished with Corian countertops and a teak and holly sole. Forward of the galley was a guest cabin, and a curving staircase at the rear of the main cabin led to the master stateroom aft. *Rao* carried only 200 gallons of water, as Robert used a watermaker on board, to maximize speed. "It's always weight against horsepower." [18]

Albert Jensen and Sons Shipyard in Friday Harbor, Washington, built the 42-foot *Ila-I* for Sam and Evelyn Perkins in 1969. The Perkins family cruised from Puget Sound to Kingcome Inlet until 1995, when *Ila-I* was sold to Tom and Mary Bess Kelly of Seattle and renamed *Conquest II*. Layout was conventional tri-cabin: two berths and a head forward; main cabin and galley amidships; twin berths, head and shower aft. Planking was yellow cedar below the waterline, Port Orford cedar above. The engine, a

"We never had a boat of our own, we had the opportunity to go boating any time. I was working all the time, and I was always aboard boats. The more boats we built, then there would be more boats we could show, and people would say, 'Well, I like this part and that part, and I want that with this.' It never did get easy, because you've got to really understand that you're building a custom boat for people, you're not selling them something off the shelf, so you're trying to fit something to their personality. You've got to know what their lifestyle is ... I mean, you don't sell a boat to a golfer. You would never be a really good golfer if you owned a boat, because you wouldn't have time!" George McQueen. [76]

below: Rao, *62 feet long, with twin V92 TA engines capable of 20 knots.* (COURTESY OF ROBERT OSBORNE)

above: Northern Light, *length 49½ ft., beam 15 ft., draft 5½ ft.* Northern Light *was built as an all-weather mission boat for the central B.C. coast, later bought by Arthur and Heather Rendell of Vancouver, B.C. Red cedar hull sheathed in gumwood, aluminum topsides. Extra large wheelhouse, and a cabin with stacked bunks for passengers in the bow. Saloon aft, with galley and dinette. Two station Wagner hydraulic steering, and one of the first auto-pilots that Wagner ever made. Four cylinder, 678 cubic inch Murphy diesel engine produced 155 hp at 1,800 rpm, turning a 36-inch four-blade propeller. Cruising speed, at 1,600 rpm, of 9.3 knots.* (ROBERT BULLER, COURTESY OF ARTHUR AND HEATHER RENDELL)

Cummins six cylinder diesel, produced a speed of 8½ knots. "A large rudder and a single, four-bladed propeller combine to make this boat easy to maneuver around docks and while underway. Because of the 2:1 reduction gear, the propeller is turning about 600 rpm at cruising speed and 250 rpm at slow idle. The hull design makes for a boat which handles rough water very well." [19]

The McQueen-built 50-foot *Mareaba* was also launched in 1969, for Basil Rae of North Vancouver, B.C. The name was changed to *Bareaba*, then to *Castaway K*. Bill and Judith Waddell bought the boat in 1996, to live aboard, and changed the name once again, to *Heather Wind*. "This boat has a wonderful layout, a walk-on swim grid with a door which leads into the cockpit, finished in mahogany and teak. The galley runs along the starboard side of the aft cabin, and the head and guest stateroom run along the port side. A step up leads to the main cabin, then there is a forward stateroom with its own head. Extra large windows through the galley and main cabin make the boat very light and airy. I can't imagine living on any other boat as we have everything here and so much room." [20]

In addition to these custom designs, there was a rapidly growing market for production boats — from the 38-foot tri-cabin cruisers (Plan No. 2583) built by Norm Nordlund in Tacoma, Washington, to fibreglass cruisers built by companies such as Rawson and Tollycraft. The Tolly 26 became a top-selling family boat, priced at $12,000 when it was introduced in 1972. Laid out by Tollefson and engineered by Monk, the Tolly 26 was functional and seaworthy, and held on to its share of the market with a reputation for looking and feeling much bigger than its size.

Some of the older yards were closing down — the slower, conventional methods of construction could not compete with plywood and fibreglass production lines. The Blanchard Boat Company was unable to recover from a fire in 1964, and was sold in 1969. The Grandy Boat Company also went out of business, after suffering devastating losses in a 1967 fire. It was no longer practical for boatbuilders to occupy expensive, highly taxed waterfront real estate, and the traditional yards gave way to "plants" located inland. Small custom boats were becoming a thing of the past, replaced by brand-name models in two-foot size increments, with slight design modifications to mark each new year.

right: "Puget Sounder" by Rawson, Inc. of Redmond, Washington, typical of the many fibreglass production boats of the 1960s and 1970s. Length 32 ft., beam 11 ft., draft 2½ ft., 130 hp Perkins diesel engine. Compact but sea-kindly, with a diesel heater, shower, swim grid, and accommodation for five. Owned by Steve Bradford, Alaska, from 1989 to 1994 and used for charters in southeast Alaska. (COURTESY OF STEVE BRADFORD)

below: Conquest II (formerly Ila-I), built in 1969 by the Jensen yard at Friday Harbor, Washington. (COURTESY OF TOM KELLY)

HEIGHTS ABOVE BASE					SHEER	W.L.9'	W.L.8'	W.L.7'	W.L.6'	CHINE	DIAG.1	DIAG.2	
SHEER	CHINE	BUT 62½	BUT 36	RABBET									
12-4-6				10-9-4	4-8-6	1-8-1	1-2-0	0-8-6			1-2-4	0	
11-9-4	7-3-0	9-0-4	5-11-4		7-6-2	5-0-2	4-4-0	3-8-4	3-0-0	3-9-7	1-10-0	3-9-0	1
11-4-0	6-0-4	6-2-4	3-11-5		8-3-6	6-9-0	6-1-7	5-7-0	4-11-4	4-11-6	2-7-0	5-0-0	2
10-10-4	5-3-0	4-7-4	3-3-2		8-6-7	7-8-0	7-2-7	6-9-0	6-2-4	5-9-4	2-10-5	5-8-0	3
10-6-6	4-8-4	3-11-4	2-11-5		8-6-0	8-0-6	7-8-6	7-4-4	7-0-0	6-6-0	2-11-6	6-0-1	4
10-3-6	4-5-0	3-8-4	2-10-4	1-11-0	8-5-5	8-2-0	7-11-3	7-8-3	7-4-7	6-9-4	3-0-0	6-1-3	5
10-1-0	4-4-0	3-8-0	2-11-6	2-1-0	8-4-0	8-1-4	7-11-0	7-8-4	7-6-0	6-10-4	2-11-0	6-1-0	6
10-0-0	4-4-0	3-9-4	3-1-6	2-4-2	8-0-6	7-11-1	7-9-0	7-7-0	7-4-0	6-9-6	2-8-2	5-11-0	7
10-0-0	4-5-1	4-0-0	3-5-2	2-9-1	7-9-0	7-7-4	7-5-4	7-3-4	7-0-7	6-7-4	2-3-5	5-7-4	8
10-0-2	4-7-0	4-3-3	3-9-7	3-3-4	7-3-4	7-1-6	7-0-8	6-10-4	6-8-2	6-3-3	1-9-4	5-2-5	9
10-0-6	4-9-0	4-7-4	4-3-4	3-11-1	6-8-4	6-7-4	6-6-4	6-5-2	6-3-0	5-10-6	1-2-2	4-9-1	10

OFFSETS IN FT, INCHES & EIGHTHS TO OUTSIDE OF FRAMES

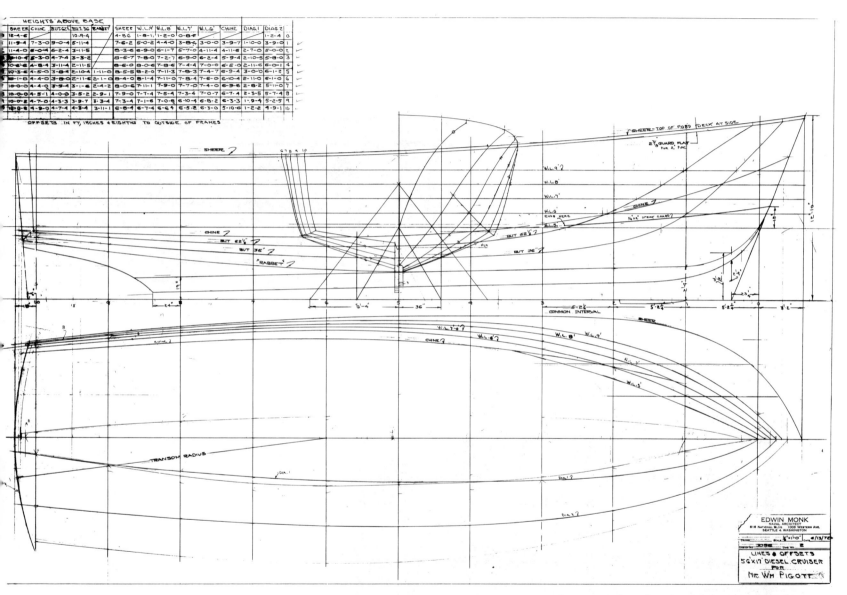

EDWIN MONK
NAVAL ARCHITECT

LINES & OFFSETS
56'X17' DIESEL CRUISER
FOR
MR WM PIGOTT

Plan No. 3096, lines and offsets of diesel cruiser, length 56 ft., beam 17 ft., for W. Pigott. (COURTESY OF ED MONK JR.)

Dutchman I, *38-foot troller launched in the late 1960s from Oak Bay Boatworks for Victoria fisherman Gus de Corte. Edge grain fir planking, oak ribs, heavy duty fir stringers, gumwood shoe. "A great sea boat, with a fantail stern which made it very buoyant in a following swell." Jim Dryburgh.* [77] (COURTESY OF JIM DRYBURGH)

CHAPTER SEVEN

SMALL SHIPS

B Y THE 1970S, the average length of the custom boat had significantly increased. The North American economy was stable and the yachting public was becoming more affluent, with most of Monk's clients ordering vessels larger than 50 feet. The tenth — and last — yacht Monk designed for himself was the 50-foot *Tryphena*, built at McQueen's Fraser River yard in 1970. *Tryphena* had a round-bottom, semi-planing hull, which Monk considered not necessarily more seaworthy than a well-designed hard-chine V, but softer riding. A lighter boat, he reasoned, rises more quickly in head seas and takes on less water, although "the really dry boat is, I think, a fable, at least from all angles of attack. At any reasonable speed the flare throws the spray out and the wind drives it back." [1]

Tryphena's 345 hp Cummins V-8 diesel produced 12 knots at 2,400 rpm, with a top speed of 16 knots. "In actuality, our modern pleasure boat power plants deliver only about ⅔ their maximum rating under continuous use. Therefore, every effort must be made to turn out a light but strong boat as a good turn of speed is desired." [2] Much effort was put into minimizing weight on *Tryphena*, including foregoing teak decks, for a saving of 500 pounds. The fuel and water tanks were aluminum, with a total capacity of only 400 gallons, and the entire hull was planked with red cedar, wedge seamed and double framed from the keel to above the bilge forward for resistance to impact. A watertight bulkhead was built underneath the forward cabin, to prevent flooding, and a well beneath the cockpit floor carried a nine hp outboard which would move the boat at three to four knots.

Paul Helman, Monk's grandson, recalled attending *Tryphena*'s launching, and joining the family for many pleasurable trips around Puget Sound. *Tryphena* was later renamed *Loki*, and was purchased by Robert and Rheta Rowland of Seattle, Washington.

"Every boat should be as light as it can reasonably be, for its purpose. With *Nika Sia* and *Tryphena*, my father's philosophy is that they were light, simple boats. He felt that if you didn't put it aboard then it didn't weigh anything, it didn't take any room, it didn't cost anything, and it never broke down. His boats were very simple, he was very pragmatic with his boats." Ed Monk Jr. [78]

"In any new design there is always the desire to come up with something new, something different. But this is not at all easily done: there is no point in being different unless difference is combined with improvement." Ed Monk. [79]

"Mother probably outfitted more boats than any other woman. Every boat that Daddy designed for himself was built with the promise, 'This will be the last one, Annie.' But, somewhere between work or dreaming at night he would come up with some 'new' idea he just had to try. And, each boat he insisted had to be sold equipped ... galley, staterooms, etc." Judy (Monk) Wade. [80]

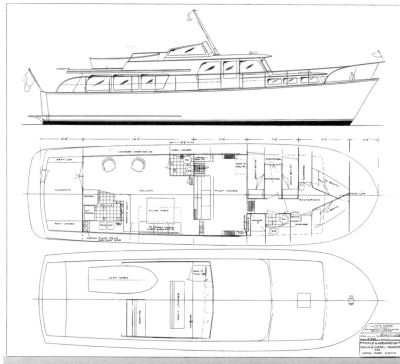

Ed and Ann Monk, aboard Tryphena, *Plan No. 2930. Length 50 ft., beam 14 ft. 6 in., draft 4 ft. Inside companionway leading from the pilothouse up to the bridge, "to make cruising much better for my first mate." Tryphena was designed to cover the miles between Puget Sound and Alaska. Above all, Monk wanted a good sea boat, with a single engine. "Admittedly it is a little harder to handle in close quarters, but it does offer simplicity. The propeller is well protected from the large amount of drift found in the Northwest, and also is protected in case of grounding (heaven forbid!)." Ed Monk.* [81] (RAY KRANTZ, COURTESY OF JUDY WADE)

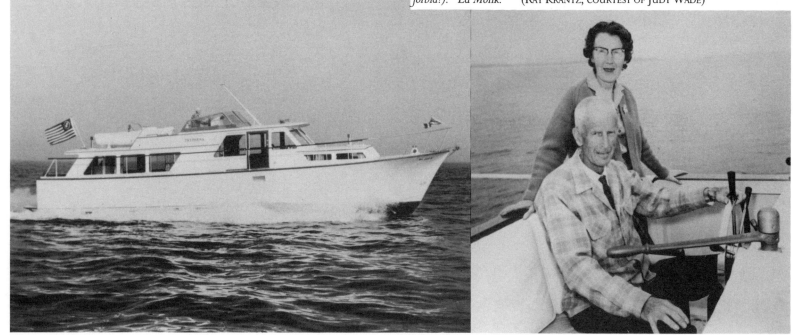

The Seventh Day Adventist Church requested a second boat in 1970, and the Nordlund Boat Company was contracted to build the 52½-foot *Messenger III*. Based out of Wrangell, Alaska, for ten years, *Messenger III* was sold in 1984 to Larry and Colleen Price and renamed *Grand Finale*. After a thorough upgrade to U. S. Coast Guard certifications, *Grand Finale* went to work for the Prices' skippered charter company, Pacific Northwest Cruises in Puget Sound.

Long-time Seattle yachtsman Norm Collins, who had previously owned a motor sailer and a Monk sedan cruiser, came up with a plan to cross the Pacific under power, collaborating with Monk on a design. His 48-foot *Ukulele Lady* was built during 1970 — with cedar planking, teak decks, and mahogany cabins — by Ed Sundquist at Lynwood, Washington, and launched the following year. *Ukulele Lady* had a semi-displacement hull, full flare, ample freeboard but a low deckhouse and bridge, a well-protected foredeck and cockpit, and nearly a ton of steel skegwork to protect the propellers from deadheads and coral reefs. She carried 800 gallons of fuel in four tanks, with three pairs of filters to serve either engine. The four cycle GM Bedfords gave a total of 292 "easy long lasting horsepower, quiet and naturally aspirated," with a cruising speed of ten knots. Many special features went into her construction: laminated safety glass, four water-tight bilge sections, extra bilge pumps, built-in flotation, and storage for a vast supply of spare parts.

Norm set out from Seattle in the summer of 1973 with his son John and two Power Squadron friends as crew. "I thought I had seen a reasonable cross section of Pacific seas in previous crossings, all the way from tremendous North Pacific winter storm seas (these experienced by ship, not small boat) on down. What we ran into from 150 to 500 miles southwest of San Francisco weren't so big, running ten to 15 or more feet, but they were cross seas, and steep and vicious in a way that none of us had seen before." With her high freeboard, good flotation aft, and low centre of gravity, *Ukulele Lady* handled herself capably; even so, Norm decided it was weather better suited to a good, solid sailboat. "For the first time ever, I was afraid. We kept on full power which helped us escape the great following cresting seas. Our strong wake helped too. It conspicuously flattened the remnants of cresters barely in time to stop them from topping our aft deck. Just one rogue wave did top us from starboard. After two days and nights we breathed easy again. But the full power had run down our fuel, and we set up the emergency square and mizzen sails and coasted down the welcome trade winds for a week to make our fuel last." [3] They had departed with 1,330 gallons of fuel, some of which was stored in

Grand Finale *(formerly* Messenger III*), length 52½ ft., beam 15 ft., draft 7 ft. Original Murphy diesel engine replaced in 1982 with a 300 hp Volvo Penta TMD-120A, giving a cruising speed of ten knots. Teak decks, 1 ⅞ inch yellow cedar planking on oak frames. Hull sheathed with one-inch ironbark above and below the waterline, to protect against damage by ice during north-coast mission work. "She hauled passengers, supplies, and mail in southeastern Alaska until 1980, when she was put up for sale. The church didn't need her any more, as roads were put in on Prince of Wales Island and the missionaries could live on land." Larry Price.* [82] (COURTESY OF LARRY AND COLLEEN PRICE)

below: Ukulele Lady *carried owner Norm Collins and crew to Hawaii, under power and sail, surviving a mid-ocean gale that took at least one other boat and two lives. She was temporarily outfitted with a small mizzenmast and a 28-foot mainmast, mounted on brackets on the foredeck, from which hung a 270-square-foot sail.* "We raised our sails for the first time when we finally hit the trades. They seemed to give us about three knots straight downwind in a 15-knot breeze, but in an agitated sea our relatively small rudders didn't give us very good steerage under sail alone. So we mostly sailed with one engine at slow cruising speed, which gave us steerage and about eight knots and four miles per gallon." *Norm Collins.* [83] (COURTESY OF NORM COLLINS)

above: Fast and elegant, Virginia-Marie *set off a new era of larger boats from McQueen in 1970. Length 60 ft., beam 16 ft., draft 4½ ft. Mahogany and cedar planking, twin 350 hp turbo Caterpillar engines, cruising speed of 18 knots. Owned by Morley and Virginia Forsyth of North Vancouver, B.C.* (COURTESY OF MORLEY FORSYTH)

extra tanks on deck, and reached Hilo, Hawaii, with 80 gallons left. After an extended cruise through the Hawaiian Islands, *Ukulele Lady* made an easy crossing home to Seattle.

Norm and Vera Collins spent many decades exploring the west coast, and kept *Ukulele Lady* at the Queen City Yacht Club on Portage Bay in Seattle, Washington. "A bunch of us retirees gather at the clubhouse each Tuesday and about 11:30 go aboard one of our boats for a three-hour lunch party," [4] Norm reported in 1997, at the age of 95.

Many of the designs that came out of the Monk office during the late 1960s and early 1970s were drawn by Ed Monk Jr. One of these was *Topaz*, modelled on the traditional lines of *Puget Pride*, an earlier design. Built for Jim and Sandy Howell of Bainbridge Island, *Topaz* was launched from the McQueen yard in 1971. In 1979 *Topaz* was bought by Ken and Donna Shields and kept at the Queen City Yacht Club. Previously, Ken and Donna had owned and restored *Ann Saunders*, Monk's first boat.

The interior of *Topaz* had a bright, clean austerity characteristic of Monk designs. Rounded corners, brass handholds, and oiled mahogany panelling were reminders that even though the owners lived aboard, this was a cruising boat. From the stern, a transom door led into a partially covered cockpit well suited to a rainy climate. The main living area was in the aft cabin, with generous seating, low tables, and a U-shaped galley with an oil stove on the starboard side. Two passageways led off from the port side: four steps down to the lower level, and four steps up to the pilothouse with the navigation and steering station, and a built-in dinette with excellent visibility. Forward, stairs curved down to the guest cabin and head with shower; the master stateroom with its queen-size, walk-around bed, was below the pilothouse.

The hull on *Topaz* was maintained so perfectly, it appeared to be illuminated from within. The owners discovered that such a finely finished vessel had a magnetic draw: a large sailboat dragging anchor in a midnight southeaster left a deep gouge along the bulwarks; a raft of poorly anchored power boats swung against one side of *Topaz*, then the other side; and a 27-foot runabout attempting a high speed turn in tight quarters drove up onto their swim grid, smashing the monogrammed teak stern. Fortunately, these and other incidents did not deter them from leaving the dock, and they spent many summers cruising the northwest.

Also in 1971, *Hinemoa* was launched from Thames Boatworks at Bowser on Vancouver Island. Cyril Thames, one of numerous builders Monk befriended along the coast, constructed several Monk-designed trollers in addition to yachts such as *Hinemoa*, *Moorea*, and *Helen Grace*.

"Up in Pender Harbour late one season, I think the fall of '72, while I was at anchor a little skiff came bounding over the water toward me and Ed Monk climbed aboard very agilely, not even waiting for the transom step or ladder. It was his first view of us and he looked the *Ukulele Lady* over, pronouncing it the kind of boat an experienced boatman should have. I'd like to think that my *Ukulele Lady* may have been the last of his 'babies' that Ed got to visit afloat like that." Norm Collins. [84]

right: Topaz, *aft cabin.* (COURTESY OF DONNA SHIELDS)

below: Topaz, *length 52 ft., beam 15½ ft., draft 7 ft. Traditionally designed with a low profile and rounded, work-boat style pilothouse. Single, turbocharged Caterpillar D-333 engine, ten knots at six gallons per hour; 1,500 gallons of fuel. Built by McQueen in 1971, owned by Ken and Donna Shields of Seattle, Washington.* (COURTESY OF ED MONK JR.)

right: Forty-foot cruiser My Ty, one of six semi-displacement hulls built from the same plans at Nicholson Boat Yard in Victoria, B.C. My Ty was launched in 1979 and completed by owners Owen and Ruth Lohr. Double-planked cedar and mahogany hull, fibreglass decks and bridge, mahogany cabin sides. Cummins 477 V-8 diesel, with a cruising speed of nine to ten knots. My Ty was kept at Capital City Yacht Club in Sidney, B.C., along with sister ship Eimut, owned by Ed and Marilyn Ackerman.
(COURTESY OF OWEN LOHR)

below: Heavy duty 52-foot cruiser Hinemoa, built by Cyril Thames in 1971.
(COURTESY OF JAMES SHANAHAN)

"I adored my father. Being the youngest in a sprawled-out family allows one to do this. There was nothing he could not fix or make right. I now know how lucky I was to have cruised the wild, uninhabited coves and islands of beautiful B.C. that are now so full of boats that everyone must stern tie. As Mother says, 'We had it at its best.' " Judy (Monk) Wade. [85]

"Ed Monk, he had a good sense of humour, a bit dry, but he could get you, all the time. We had a lot of fun. He worked with his hands right from the beginning; he understood boats. We could talk about it, you know, in planning a boat. He would have a couple of rollers on his desk, and his rule, and he'd say, 'Yes, that'll be all right, that'll balance.' Now you've got computers that will tell if a design is going to go or not. But Ed knew. He had just a terrific feel. He was quite a guy." George McQueen. [86]

"To me, Ed Monk brought us into the modern pleasure boat age with his beautification of our pleasure boats. Before the war, and Ed Monk, they were boxy or cluttered. Ed Monk introduced smooth, pleasing lines that have dominated ever since. As you know, he also championed lighter construction. 'Every pound weighs her down,' he always said." Norm Collins, *Ukulele Lady*. [87]

The 52-foot *Hinemoa* was designed for long-distance cruising with a single Cummins VT8-370 engine, 860 gallons of fuel and 600 gallons of water. The master stateroom was forward, the aft stateroom had twin berths, and the main living area was amidships. With a full standing-headroom workbench in the engine room, washer and dryer, built-in vacuum cleaner and complete entertainment system, *Hinemoa* was a comfortable liveaboard for James Shanahan of Seattle, who owned the boat until 1996.

Throughout his 70s Monk commuted daily from Bainbridge Island to his office in the National Building, catching the 7:10 ferry in the morning and the 5:10 home. He would light a fire and sit down and read in the evenings; he enjoyed books about Franklin D. Roosevelt, whom he greatly admired. "He was always going to retire, but never did," according to his daughter, Judy Wade. [5] He had lived a quiet life, honouring the work ethic that had brought his father from Plymouth, England, to America, building a new country. "My father was of the old school," said Ed Monk Jr. "If people came with a job, he said yes." [6]

Monk's long career came to an end when he was 79; after a short bout of influenza, he died on January 21, 1973. A memorial service was held at St. Barnabas Episcopal Church, on Bainbridge Island, to which he and his wife belonged. His passing was mourned by the local community; he had been active in the Seattle and Queen City yacht clubs, the Society Of Naval Architects and Marine Engineers, and had been a founding member of Northwest Marine Industries.

Obituaries were published in newspapers and boating magazines across the country. "Mr. Monk designed thousands of boats and was highly regarded as an innovator and consultant as well," noted the *Bainbridge Review*. "A 'Monk design' is a strong selling point for prospective boat buyers and his designs are known all over the world." [7]

"He was humble, with the precision of the engineer but with the eye of the artist," wrote Gordon Jones, in *WoodenBoat* magazine, remembering the first time he had met Monk, while apprenticing at the Grandy Boat Company in the 1940s. [8]

"He will be missed by many friends who benefited from his marine philosophies," wrote the editor of *SEA and Pacific Motor Boat*. "He never discouraged people in their quest for certain design ideas. But when he felt the idea was not a good one, he had an unobtrusive way of bringing the skipper around to better alternatives and the prevention of fiascos. Because of just these gentle ways in accomplishing his leadership, his friendships grew to immense proportions." [9]

The design firm continued under the direction of Ed Monk Jr., who shared much of his father's approach to his work and gradually developed a specialty in pleasure boat design. Jack Sarin, who had come from Stephens Marine in Stockton, California, and had been his father's assistant for the past six years, became responsible for the workboats. Their business expanded throughout the 1970s, and Jack Sarin eventually left to set up his own office as a naval architect. There were inevitable changes: with rising labour costs and a scarcity of prime boat lumber, fibreglass had become the construction material of choice. Shipyards in the Orient were taking over the production of mid-sized boats, particularly the tri-cabin style which Monk had pioneered. Tollycraft continued to put out their highly reputable line, with Ed Monk Jr. designing the hulls until 1988, when the company was sold. Tolly Tollefson commissioned his distinctive, blue-hulled *Tolly* and then retired, cruising to his favourite destinations on the Washington and B.C. coasts.

During the mid-1970s, Earl Wakefield supervised the construction of the 73-foot power boat *Myirma* for Jim Coulas of Chicago. Built out of aluminum, *Myirma* took 2½ years to complete and was used for cruising Lake Michigan and the inland waterways to Florida.

The luxurious, 70-foot *Shel-Lor* was built by McQueen in 1974, commissioned by Clarke Simpkins and later owned by Warren and Anne Whyte of North Vancouver, B.C. The spacious bridge deck on *Shel-Lor* provided enough upholstered seating for a party; the lower deck, aft, was furnished with table and chairs for outdoor dining. Couches, coffee tables, lamps, and paintings filled the main living area, which was surrounded by large windows. The eating area was forward, down several steps, along with a galley better equipped than many new condominiums. Guest accommodation was in two cabins in the bow, with stacked berths. A passageway led below the main deck, between spotless, carpeted, twin engine rooms, past the laundry and storage area, to the master cabin aft. *Shel-Lor* was refurbished during the 1990s, and used extensively by the Whytes for cruising the Gulf Islands and Desolation Sound.

The pilothouse configuration that worked so well with *Nika Sia* and Bob Gibson's 51-foot *Gibson Gal* continued to be adapted to many newer vessels. *Venn Skip* (Norwegian for friend ship), 54 feet long with a 15-foot beam, was launched from the McQueen yard in the early 1970s. Outfitted with twin 300 Cummins diesel engines, *Venn Skip* cruised at 12 knots, using 13 gallons per hour; the top speed of 19 knots doubled the fuel consumption. In addition to an oil furnace, *Venn Skip* had a small, cast-iron wood-burning stove in the main lounge, for instant dry heat. *Venn Skip* was

Gibson Gal, length 75 ft., beam 18 ft., draft 4 ft., twin 425 V-8 GM diesel engines, running speed 15 knots. Mahogany hull below the waterline, red cedar above; fir keel with gumwood stem; teak decks; fibreglass over plywood cabin sides and tops. Main deck with wheelhouse, settees, galley, and dining area. Lower deck with four staterooms, three heads, engine room and lazarette.

"By 1970 Ed had been designing larger vessels, and we ordered our 63-footer, our third Gibson Gal, taking delivery from McQueen in 1973. This was a beautiful vessel, and seemed so spacious and comfortable that I started making notes for an even larger Gibson Gal. By 1979 Ed Jr. had the plans ready for our final Gibson Gal — to be 75 feet — and indeed the finest vessel I have ever owned. This vessel was commissioned in May 1981 and today is in better condition than ever. We have logged miles upon miles up and down this coast, and while this vessel was one of the last all-wood-hulled vessels built by McQueen, it is admired by all boaters, and remains a credit to Ed Monk Sr. and his son, Ed Monk Jr." Robert Gibson. [88] (COURTESY OF ROBERT GIBSON)

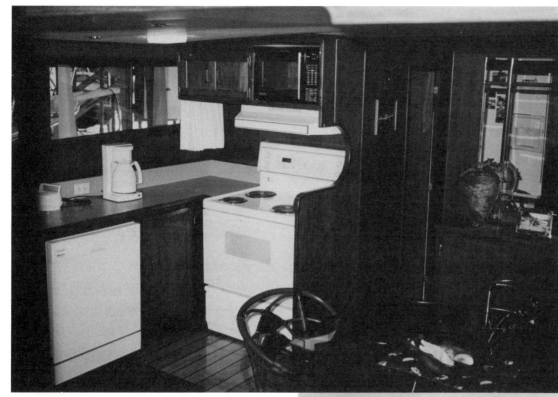

above: Shel-Lor, *galley.* (COURTESY OF WARREN WHYTE)

right: Shel-Lor, *length 70 ft., beam 18 ft., draft 4 ft., 52.05 registered tons. Twin turbo-charged Cummins diesels, cruising speed of 13 to 14 knots. Carvel-planked cedar hull, teak decks, fibreglass over plywood house and bridge. 600 gallons fuel, 25 gallons-per-hour watermaker, recessed halogen lighting, three televisions, and a bowthruster with electronic controls for docking by the owners, who handled the boat themselves.* (COURTESY OF WARREN WHYTE)

Tokalon, length 42 ft. 6 in., beam 14 ft. 2 in., draft 3 ft. Cummins 210 diesel. Built by Harry Runer, owned by Hugh and Lisa Gordon of Sidney, B.C.

"Ed Monk certainly deserves to live on in the memory of those who built or own one of his boats. I became attracted to Ed's boats when I was cruising in my first boat, a 23-foot Brandlemeyer that I built in 1960. Ed's boats were solid looking and as I found out later, that was the way they were designed. I went to Ed's office in Seattle in 1964 and selected a plan for a 32½ foot boat, *La Serena*, which I built and launched in 1967. That meeting with Ed Monk was a great experience. Here was a kind, honest, caring man who would spend as much time with me, an amateur builder, as he would with anyone else. He was always there to answer questions and give helpful advice.

"After selling *La Serena* in 1972, I again contacted Ed for a plan for the *Tokalon*. Ed died just before I went down to pick up the plans, so I received them from his son who also dealt with me fairly. *Tokalon* was built on a lot off Holland Avenue in Victoria, B.C., starting in 1973, and launched in October 1976. It was a joy working with Ed's plans which carried no mistakes. After lofting the boat from his table of offsets, I found them to be 'bang on.' The hull was planked with 1⅛ inch red cedar on 1⅜ inch by 1¾ inch oak ribs. The planks were ripped to four-inch widths and scarfed to make a continuous length, thus eliminating butt blocks. The grooves were routed out to form an 11½ degree included angle, using a custom-made carbide cutter. Cutting wedges in five, six, and seven foot lengths, they were glued and driven in hard all around the boat including the bottom. It was a great satisfaction to me to be able to do this when people said it couldn't be done. Some 20 gallons of UF 109 went into the glueing. The cabin sides were made of the same material as the hull, with plywood fingers put in the edge joints. Following Ed's plans made for an extremely solid boat, good enough to withstand a six-foot drop with minimal damage on the first launch attempt when the crane slings slipped off. After launching, the boat floated on the waterline that Ed designed. The soft chine and sharp entry made for a smooth and comfortable ride in all seas. I still think they are among the best-looking boats on the water." Harry Runer. [89]

Emslie "Bim" Clark of North Vancouver, B.C., began construction on the 40-foot *Binadac II* in 1973; she was launched in 1979. Powered by a Perkins 165 hp T6-354 diesel, cruising speed of 8½ knots at 2,000 rpm. Mahogany strip-planked over bent-oak frames, fastened with silicone bronze screws. Distinctive brightwork transom found on many boats of this type: curved and raked, finished with ¾ inch wedge-seamed mahogany. Tri-cabin layout with command bridge; two bunks forward, ample seating (including a sofa/day bed) in the wheelhouse, aft cabin with large galley, oil stove and dinette. Bim and his wife, Nancy, have fond memories of the free-standing, wood-burning fireplace in *Binadac II*'s main cabin, where they entertained friends and family. "The good-sized rudder makes for a great difference in handling. Head seas and beam seas are okay but a stern sea makes for that extra steering. Has been cruised extensively in northern and southern islands, and used all year round." Bim Clark. [90]

left: Tokalon. (COURTESY OF LISA GORDON)

below: Binadac II. (COURTESY OF BIM CLARK)

A modern classic, the 47-foot *Anderson Cove* was completed in 1994 by owners Warren and Carol Heard. Master stateroom and head forward; curving stairs leading up to the large pilothouse with a steering station, fully equipped galley and raised dinette with remote control auto-pilot; steps down and aft to a main living area which opened onto the cockpit. "Everything in the boat is domestic size — the custom king-size bed, the shower stall, vanities, galley appliances. The galley stove is a 30-inch gas range, converted to propane. The three-way fridge, in a gas-tight compartment, has a plenum which would direct any leaks to the outside of the hull. Dishwasher, microwave/convection oven, instant hot water, Corian countertops, lazy susans, cupboards built into the stairs — every inch of space is utilized. The bed is on a hydraulic lift — you press a button and up she goes, for storage. Standard-size clothes closets and drawers, all heated by hot water pipes. All quartz halogen lighting, except for fluorescent lights over the mirrors in the heads. The pumps in the shower are vacu-flush toilet pumps, will never clog. The oil-fired heating system is absolutely smokeless. We used heater hose, one-inch, the best you can get, and stretched 135 feet of it around the boat. Then I insulated every square inch of it. All the heat is retained — it heats the domestic hot water, and the engine. The engine, when it is running, reverses through the heat exchanger, heats the hot water, and heats the boat." Warren Heard. [91]

taken north for many summers by owner Kaare Norgaard, who started out boating on the North Sea.

Phil Barron of East Sooke, B.C., built five versions of Monk's pilot-house design: *Timisit II*, *Alexaire*, *Bos-Sea Lady*, *Anderson Cove*, and *Joyce Marie*. The 47-foot *Anderson Cove* was commissioned by Warren and Carol Heard of Sidney, B.C. On the transom section of the blueprints for *Anderson Cove* were the handwritten names of the boats — ranging from 44 to 55 feet — built from the same plans. "This is a soft chine, light displacement hull. It flattens out towards the back, and is much shallower draft than a heavy displacement hull, drawing a little over four feet. The keel line is cut away to form a skeg so the shaft is open, with a strut, much like you do with a planing hull, but the skeg carries on to the back and the bottom of the strut to protect the propeller from logs. So you have an open shaft with a very thin strut, which is meant to gulp more water and go faster." Warren shopped all over the coast for a used engine, finally tracking down an 8 V-71 TI Detroit diesel in a Seattle warehouse. "It's more horsepower than what was required, but the dimensions were right, and so was the price. We cruise at 9½ to 10 knots at 1,600 rpm, burning around 4½ gallons an hour." [10]

Warren assisted Phil Barron in planking the hull, using ¼ inch fir below the waterline, western red cedar above. The 38½ foot planks were cut from a single fir log, weighing over 12 tons, which came from a dry-land sorting yard on Vancouver Island's west coast. The ribs were 1¼ inch by 2½ inch white oak, strong, clear-grained, and resistant to rot. Deck beams were yellow cedar, and the transom was framed in solid yellow cedar and covered in ¾ inch marine plywood, with an outer surface of ¾ inch teak. The waterline was wedge-seamed, caulked from the waterline down. More than 7,000 silicone bronze screws were used to fasten the hull. "I cut all the plugs on a little drill press out in my workshop, from scraps, and they were the wrong size," said Warren. "The counter sink that I was using at the time came from Boeing Surplus in Seattle, and it must have been metric or something — just that hair difference in size, and it was meant to counter sink for aluminum, for aircraft construction. So I had to start all over again." [11] The boat became a floating workshop, completed after five years of work by Warren and his wife.

During the late 1960s and early 1970s, Monk's designs for multi-purpose, fibreglass trollers such as the 46-foot "Bluefin" and the 52-foot "Seamaster" proved their worth among fishermen in the northwest. Philbrook's Shipyard in Sidney, B.C., built four from the Seamaster mould: *Miss Pacific*, *Chaperone*, *Windrift*, and *Pacific Concept*, and dozens more were

above: Anderson Cove, *elegant aft saloon.* (COURTESY OF WARREN AND CAROL HEARD)

right: Anderson Cove, *passing through Sansum Narrows.* (HELEN BUCK, COURTESY OF WARREN AND CAROL HEARD)

EDWIN MONK & SON
NAVAL ARCHITECTS

616 National Building
Seattle, Washington 98104, U.S.A.

October 19, 1972

Mr. E. C. Clark
2575 Bendale Road
North Vancouver, B.C., Canada

Dear Mr. Clark:

First re the wheel - the boat should weigh about 19,000# and with
160 h.p. our chart shows 15 miles, or 13 knots top. With 160 h.p.
@2400 and 2-1 reduction the diameter should be 24'. Using 30%
slip the pitch 19".

We find the modern stainless steel shaft considerably cheaper and
it is much stronger, I have it in our own boat which is kept in
salt water and have had no trouble with electrolysis. Using
17-4 ph. the dia. should be 1-1/2".

If it were my boat I would caulk the first strip not, however,
until bottom was all planked. I would suggest the strips be
about 2" over all, perhaps you can get 2" rough and come out with
1-7/8 when ripped.

Am quite sure we can balance your wheel house idea along with the
tank locations.

Presume you will use the engine fuel return to fill the stove oil
tank but would like to await the final arrangement before locating
it.

Three Martlets, *length 35 ft., beam 12½ ft., draft 3½ ft. Built by Jim Dryburgh of Victoria, B.C., in 1979, named after the Dryburgh family crest. Semi-displacement hull, flat at the stern, with hard chine; 120 hp Ford diesel, cruising speed of nine to ten knots. Double stateroom and head forward, spacious main cabin, large partially covered cockpit suited to socializing and sport fishing.* (COURTESY OF JIM DRYBURGH)

Telephone (206) 682-4317

(COURTESY OF BIM CLARK)

built throughout Puget Sound. Pete Peterson of Sidney commissioned *Miss Pacific* in 1978, "a very good sea boat for its size," [12] which he took offshore for tuna, salmon, and halibut, in addition to packing herring.

The Philbrook's mould was later used for the trollers *Seaborn I*, built by Phil Seaborn, and *Royal Spirit*, built by Phil Barron. Laurie and Bonnie Derrien of Sidney adapted the design to suit a liveaboard cruiser, and rented the mould to lay up the hull for their *Raincoast Spirit*, launched in 1992. The interior of *Raincoast Spirit* was finished with cedar and mahogany. The large wheelhouse also held the galley, to starboard, and a built-in dinette to port. There were two guest cabins forward, and a spacious master stateroom below the wheelhouse, with a full-size bathtub and head. The aft cabin opened onto a partially covered cockpit and boarding platform.

The hull for the 58-foot *Hi-Dad* was also from the same mould, with an aluminum superstructure and layout designed by Pat Bray. Commissioned by Rick Cockburn of Vancouver, B.C., who had previously circled the Pacific Ocean in a 45-foot converted troller, *Hi-Dad* carried 3,500 gallons of fuel and had a range of 7,000 miles. The Gardner 8L-B diesel, with a running speed of 8½ knots at 850 rpm, was housed in a roomy, watertight engine room with two starters and a dry-stack exhaust. The boat displaced 55 tons; the bow was reinforced with three feet of concrete, and three-inch-thick stainless-steel plating bolstered the stem and keel. In 1996 *Hi-Dad* put in a star performance, in the movie "Free Willy 2."

Hi-Dad, and similar vessels derived from commercial fishing-boat hulls, were examples of the growing interest in offshore-capable yachts. Since the early 1970s naval architects such as James Krogen, Steve Seaton, and Jeff Leishman have been building on the work of Monk, William Garden, Al Mason, Weston Farmer and Walter McInnis of Eldredge-McInnis, designer of the 98-foot *Speejacks* in the 1920s, the first power boat to circumnavigate the world. Jeff Leishman produced the "Nordhavn" series with his brother James, who wrote a revised edition of Robert Beebe's *Voyaging Under Power* in 1994.

Roy Parkinson of Park Isle Marine, based near Sooke, B.C., used the Seamaster mould for the 57-foot *Fine Romance*, commissioned in 1997 by owners from Newport Beach, California. Engineered by Parkinson, with a superstructure designed by naval architect Gregory Marshall, *Fine Romance* was equipped for a five-year world cruise. The full-displacement solid laminate hull was heavily reinforced, with watertight collision bulkheads and moulded lead ballast in the keel. The fuel-efficient Caterpillar D-33306 B engine, rated at 190 hp continuous, produced 11 knots at 1,800

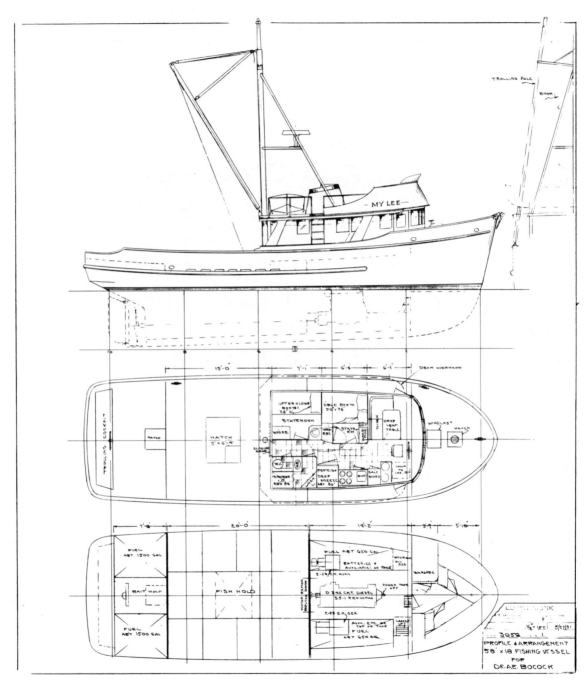

Plan No. 3056, 58-foot My Lee. (COURTESY OF ED MONK JR.)

left: All-weather cruiser Raincoast Spirit, *built by owners Laurie and Bonnie Derrien, Sidney, B.C. Length 52 ft., beam 16 ft., draft 7 ft., displacement 46 tons. Carried 1,000 Imperial gallons water, 1,500 Imperial gallons fuel. Cruising speed of eight knots with a 180 hp Detroit 6 V71 diesel, using 3 ½ to 4 gallons per hour. (*MARY SEABORN, COURTESY OF LAURIE AND BONNIE DERRIEN)

right: Fine Romance, *length 57 ft., beam 16 ft. 4 in., draft 6 ft. 4 in., dry displacement 108,000 pounds. First in the "Royal Passagemaker" series by Park Isle Marine, Sooke, B.C.* (PAINTING BY DWIGHT LOCKHART, COURTESY OF ROY PARKINSON)

rpm, an increase from the standard ten knots with the addition of a bulb on the bow. Tested extensively on commercial vessels in Pacific Northwest waters, the bulbous bow was shown to decrease both pitch and water resistance, with a saving in operating costs. For roll reduction, essential on an ocean passage, the hull was outfitted with activated fins controlled by a gyro unit.

Fine Romance carried 1,100 gallons of fresh water aboard, in addition to a 500-gallon-per-day watermaker. Fuel capacity was 2,700 Imperial gallons, giving a range of 5,000 miles. The 90 hp auxiliary engine had its own shaft and folding propeller, for trolling or emergency use, and the computerized electrical system was engineered to handle a variety of services worldwide. Two 2,500 watt inverters and large-capacity deep cycle batteries supplemented the 20 kw generator, which was outfitted with a split exhaust system to minimize noise. "With the battery bank on this boat, two people could sit at anchor and have all the amenities of home for a week." [13]

The Portuguese bridge allowed for safe watch-keeping at sea, as well as protecting the pilothouse. Wrap-around seating was built into the upper bridge, and the aft deck was outfitted with a barbecue, refrigerator, icemaker, sink and hot tub, in addition to the dinghy and crane. The workshop, utility room, galley and entertainment centre contained all the amenities of home, including a 45-inch television. No wood was used on the exterior, for ease of maintenance; main cabins were finished in maple, and the three staterooms were finished in white ash.

In the early 1980s the Monk design firm moved from Seattle to Bainbridge Island, where three generations of the family had made their home. Working exclusively with two yards, Nordlund and McQueen, they produced custom fibreglass power boats for an international clientele. In addition, Ed Monk Jr. drew the designs for Ocean Alexander, a line of luxury yachts built in the Orient. Technical advances in yacht construction required flawless teamwork between the builder and designer, with the aid of computer software. "The kind of plans that we have to do today are so much more complex than my father had to do," explained Ed Monk Jr., in 1997, "and because of that, we only do a handful of boats a year." [14] Detailed drawings illustrated every aspect of structural, mechanical and electrical installations, whereas originally a set of plans consisted of four hand-drawn sheets: outboard profile and arrangement; inboard profile; lines drawing and offsets; and interior sections. Nevertheless, the hulls were still tested using scale models, as Monk had done on the shore of Lake Union many years before.

These boats are part of a design legacy which began with *Nan*, Plan No. 1, and continued through six decades. Drawing on the skills of his forefathers, Monk led the way in fusing simplicity with function and beauty of line. "He knew how boats should be built," said Norman Blanchard. [15] He passed that knowledge on to his son and to countless others inspired by his work. His boats will be treasured, rebuilt, and — most of all — allow their owners to follow their "spirit of adventure," as he wished.

ENDNOTES TO TEXT

CHAPTER ONE: FOUR GENERATIONS OF SHIPWRIGHTS

1. Norman Blanchard, telephone interview with author, December 4, 1996
2. Ibid.
3. Josephine (Monk) Helman's memoirs, from Paul Helman's personal correspondence with author, March 4, 1997
4. Isabel (Monk) Van Valey, personal correspondence with author, February 25, 1997
5. Bob Hansen, "Edwin Monk," *Popular Boating*, March 1962, p.124
6. "A New 52-Foot 16-Knot Stock Cruiser," *Pacific Motor Boat*, March 1929, p.46
7. E. G. Monk, "A Fast 25-Foot Sport Cruiser," *Pacific Motor Boat*, June 1930, p.35
8. "Barrymore Orders 120-Footer," *Pacific Motor Boat*, December 1929, p.45
9. "*Maydo*," *Pacific Motor Boat*, September 1931, p.13
10. Doug Egan, personal correspondence with author, November 18, 1997
11. Bob Hansen, "Edwin Monk," *Popular Boating*, March 1962, p.122
12. Steve Bunnell, "Northwest Yachting Legends: Ed Monk Sr.," *Northwest Yachting*, September 1991, p.38
13. E.G. Monk, "A 30-Foot Express Cruiser," *Pacific Motor Boat*, April 1930, p.30
14. E.G. Monk, "Stowing The Dinghy," *Pacific Motor Boat*, December 1930, p.13
15. Edwin Monk, "Dodging Your Naval Architect," *Pacific Motor Boat*, July 1931, p.18
16. Edwin Monk, "How To Build A Half-Model," *Yachting*, December 1933, p.54
17. Edwin Monk, "Why A Better Time To Build?" *Pacific Motor Boat*, August 1933, p.14

CHAPTER TWO: A CAREER BEGINS

1. Josephine (Monk) Helman's memoirs, from Paul Helman's personal correspondence with author, March 4, 1997
2. Paul Helman, "The *Nan*," personal correspondence with author, March 4, 1997
3. Bob Hansen, "Edwin Monk," *Popular Boating*, March 1962, p.122
4. Edwin Monk, *Small Boat Building*, Charles Scribner's Sons, New York, 1934, p.1

5. Ibid., p.51
6. "Construction Progress And Outlook," *Pacific Motor Boat*, December 1934, p.7
7. Ed Monk Jr., interview with author, December 9, 1997
8. Edwin Monk, "Designed For Living," *Pacific Motor Boat*, December 1941, p.8
9. "Big Times Ahead," *Pacific Motor Boat*, October 1936, p.28
10. Edwin Monk, " 'Ebb-Tide' — A Neat Little Centerboarder," *Pacific Motor Boat*, March 1936, p.10
11. Edwin Monk, "The 1937 Edition Of The Sloop 'Brevity'," *Pacific Motor Boat*, January 1937, p.25
12. Edwin Monk, *Modern Boat Building*, Charles Scribner's Sons, New York, 1939 (1949 Edition) p.3
13. Ibid., p.21
14. Edwin Monk, "A Practical Boat House Pays Dividends," *Pacific Motor Boat*, February 1940, p.40
15. Josephine (Monk) Helman's memoirs, from Paul Helman's personal correspondence with author, March 4, 1997

CHAPTER THREE: TOWBOATS AND TROLLERS

1. R. F. "Tolly" Tollefson, interview with author, May 28, 1997
2. "30-Foot Towboat For Alaska," *Pacific Motor Boat*, date unknown
3. "New 154-Foot Vessels For Cable Work," *Pacific Motor Boat*, August 1943, p.16
4. Edwin Monk, "A New Type Of Stern Speeds The *Heron*," *Pacific Motor Boat*, November 1940, p.29
5. Anne Vipond, "*Mariner III*," *Pacific Yachting*, June 1991, p.59
6. "New 62-Foot Cruiser For Adolf Schmidt," *Pacific Motor Boat*, May 1941, p.28
7. Edwin Monk, "A New Type Of Fast Troller For 1940," *Pacific Motor Boat*, February 1940, p.15
8. "Twin 'Drag' Boats For Astoria, Puget Sound," *Pacific Motor Boat*, July 1941, p.25
9. "We'll Take Six Just Like Her — RCAF," *Pacific Motor Boat*, August 1944, p.16
10. Bill Osborne, personal correspondence with author, February 17, 1997
11. Don Bostrum, interview with author, January 17, 1997
12. Lee Morris, personal correspondence with author, January 20, 1997
13. Vern Sampson, personal correspondence with author, October 6, 1997
14. John Parkyn, personal correspondence with author, October 29, 1997

CHAPTER FOUR: THE POST-WAR BOOM

1. Edwin Monk, "Pleasure Craft — How Many, What Kind, How Soon," *Pacific Motor Boat*, March 1944, p.12
2. "New Army Types Delivered Mark Another Busy Month For Builders," *Pacific Motor Boat*, May 1944, p.24
3. Edwin Monk, "Pleasure Craft — How Many, What Kind, How Soon," *Pacific Motor Boat*, March 1944, p.12
4. *Pacific Motor Boat*, December 1946, p.17

5. Ed Monk Jr., interview with author, December 9, 1997
6. "New 50-Footer Features Ingenious Arrangement," *Pacific Motor Boat*, December 1946, p.63
7. Verda Bartlett, "The Spirit Of Adventure," *Motor Boat*, December 1952, p.13
8. Bob Hansen, "Edwin Monk," *Popular Boating*, March 1962, p.124
9. Ibid.
10. Earl Wakefield, interview with author, January 10, 1998
11. Rosie Atkinson, "Hitting The Sawdust Trail," *Nor'westing*, August 1989, p.18
12. Edwin Monk, "*Spray*," *Brochure Of Pleasure Boat Design*, Port Madison Press
13. Gordon Nickells, interview with author, January 31, 1997
14. Ibid.
15. R.L. "Bob" Stewart, personal correspondence with author, February 21, 1997
16. Ibid.
17. Bill Szabo, personal correspondence with author, March 24, 1997
18. R.L. "Bob" Stewart, personal correspondence with author, February 21, 1997
19. Edwin Monk, "Vagabond II," *Pacific Motor Boat*, June 1935, p.22
20. Don Sandall, personal correspondence with author, June 17, 1997
21. John King, personal correspondence with author, December 12, 1996
22. Wayne Robinson, personal correspondence with author, December 15, 1996
23. Dan Moldenhauer, personal correspondence with author, March 15, 1997
24. Edwin Monk, "Pleasure Craft — How Many, What Kind, How Soon," *Pacific Motor Boat*, March 1944, p.13

CHAPTER FIVE: "SOMETHING A LITTLE NEW IN HULL DESIGN"

1. Edwin Monk, "Power Cruiser Types," *Yachting*, January 1954, p.106
2. Ibid., p.107
3. Ibid.
4. Edwin Monk, "A Vancouver Island Cruise," *Yachting*, December 1952, p.41
5. Dave Gerr, *The Nature Of Boats*, International Marine Publishing, Camden, Maine, 1992, p.138
6. Ibid., p.137
7. Ibid., p.138
8. Edwin Monk, "A Vancouver Island Cruise," *Yachting*, December 1952, p.41
9. Edwin Monk, "Power Cruiser Types," *Yachting*, January 1954, p.107
10. Edwin Monk, "A Vancouver Island Cruise," *Yachting*, December 1952, p.42
11. R.F. "Tolly" Tollefson, interview with author, May 28, 1997
12. Ron Kondrat, personal correspondence with author, August 24, 1997

13. Robert P. Beebe, *Voyaging Under Power*, Seven Seas Press, New York, 1975, cover
14. Ibid., p.132
15. Ibid., p.136
16. Edwin Monk, "A Designer Plans His Own Boat," *Yachting*, March 1956, p.65
17. Ibid.
18. Robert Gibson, personal correspondence with author, May 12, 1997
19. Edwin Monk, "Swordfish," *Brochure Of Pleasure Boat Design*, Port Madison Press
20. Ibid., "Scat"
21. Ibid., "Carowil"

CHAPTER SIX: PROGRESS ... IN STYLE
1. Edwin Monk, "You And Your Naval Architect," *Yachting*, December 1963, p.41
2. Bob Hansen, "Edwin Monk," *Popular Boating*, March 1962, p.124
3. Edwin Monk, "Weight And The Motor Boat," *Yachting*, January 1955, p.118
4. Edwin Monk, "What Shape The Hull," *Yachting*, June 1969, p.70
5. Edwin Monk, *Brochure Of Pleasure Boat Design*, Port Madison Press
6. Edwin Monk, "You And Your Naval Architect," *Yachting*, December 1963, p.41
7. Robert Osborne, interview with author, February 14, 1997
8. Ed Monk Jr., interview with author, December 9, 1997
9. Edwin Monk, "Vancouver: The West Side Story," *SEA and Pacific Motor Boat*, March 1965, pp.47-49
10. Ray Krantz, "Ed Monk, World Famous Seattle Naval Architect," *Nor'westing*, March 1970, p.16
11. Edwin Monk, "The Offshore Cruiser," *Yachting*, March 1966, p.75
12. Edwin Monk, "Anti-Roll Devices," *Yachting*, March 1971, p.64
13. Edwin Monk, *Brochure Of Pleasure Boat Design*, Port Madison Press
14. Ibid.
15. Edwin Monk, "*Nika Sia*," *SEA and Pacific Motor Boat*, February 1965, p.122
16. Ibid., p.122
17. Edwin Monk, *Brochure Of Pleasure Boat Design*, Port Madison Press
18. Robert Osborne, interview with author, February 14, 1997
19. Tom Kelly, personal correspondence with author, March 12, 1997
20. Judith Waddell, personal correspondence with author, June 14, 1997

CHAPTER SEVEN: SMALL SHIPS
1. Edwin Monk, "A Man And His Boat," *Yachting*, December 1972, p.65

2. Edwin Monk, "Monk Describes A New 50-Footer: His Own," *SEA and Pacific Motor Boat*, February 1971, p.45
3. Norm Collins, "To Hawaii Under Power ... And A Little Sail," *Yachting*, May 1974, p.124
4. Norm Collins, personal correspondence with author, October 6, 1997
5. Jo Bailey-Cummings, "*Sea Witch* Turns 50," *Nor'westing*, November 1989, p.18
6. Ed Monk Jr., interview with author, December 9, 1997
7. *Bainbridge Review*, Vol. 73, No. 4, January 24, 1973
8. Gordon Jones, "Forget The Alehouses," *WoodenBoat*, Number 10, May/June 1973, p.70
9. "Naval Architect Edwin Monk Dies At Age 79," *SEA and Pacific Motor Boat*, March 1973
10. Warren Heard, interview with author, April 10, 1997
11. Ibid.
12. Pete Peterson, personal correspondence with author, May 11, 1997
13. Roy Parkinson, interview with author, November 29, 1997
14. Ed Monk Jr., interview with author, December 9, 1997
15. Norman Blanchard, telephone interview with author, December 4, 1996

ENDNOTES TO CAPTIONS AND SIDEBARS

1. Josephine (Monk) Helman's memoirs, from Paul Helman's personal correspondence with author, March 4, 1997
2. E.G. Monk, "A Pram Dinghy," *Pacific Motor Boat*, February 1930, p.13
3. Edwin Monk, *Small Boat Building*, p.85
4. Edwin Monk, *Small Boat Building*, p.59
5. Edwin Monk, "Designed For Living," *Pacific Motor Boat*, December 1941, p.8
6. Paul Helman, personal correspondence with author, May 12, 1997
7. Diane Anderson, personal correspondence with author, April 15, 1997
8. Log of the *Nan*, courtesy of Paul Helman
9. Eric Finn, personal correspondence with author, May 14, 1997
10. Log of the *Nan*, courtesy of Paul Helman
11. Tom Kincaid, personal correspondence with author, February 11, 1997
12. Hugh Garrett, personal correspondence with author, November 1, 1997
13. Don Sandall, personal correspondence with author, June 17, 1997
14. Edwin Monk, *Small Boat Building*, p.45
15. J. Ellsworth Jensen, from U.S. Monk Club records, January 18, 1993
16. John Bailey, personal correspondence with author, September 15, 1997
17. Log of the *Nan*, courtesy of Paul Helman
18. "New 28-Foot Towboat For Army," *Pacific Motor Boat*, April 1943, p.22

19. Norm Collins, personal correspondence with author, October 6, 1997
20. John Beveridge, personal correspondence with author, October 17, 1997
21. Mary Edna Ross, "Surprise Cruise To Gardner Canal," *SEA and Pacific Motor Boat*, January 1957, p.85
22. Claude Bigler, personal correspondence with author, June 15, 1997
23. Henry Clark, interview with author, May 4, 1997
24. Lee Morris, personal correspondence with author, January 20, 1997
25. Don Bostrum, interview with author, January 17, 1997
26. Vern Sampson, personal correspondence with author, October 6, 1997
27. John Parkyn, personal correspondence with author, October 29, 1997
28. Fred Bailey, personal correspondence with author, August 21, 1997
29. Earl Wakefield, interview with author, January 10, 1998
30. Verda Bartlett, "*Holiday*'s Third Trip Around Vancouver Island," *SEA and Pacific Motor Boat*, October 1959, p.92
31. Vic Griffin, interview with author, November 1, 1996
32. Earl Wakefield, interview with author, January 10, 1998
33. Ibid.
34. Rosie Atkinson, "The Stuff Of Which Dreams Are Made," *Nor'westing*, December 1989, p.27
35. Maurice Green, telephone interview with author, January 29, 1997
36. George and Betty Hansen, personal correspondence with author, October 30, 1997
37. Don Sandall, personal correspondence with author, June 17, 1997
38. Carl Montford, personal correspondence with author, October 7, 1997
39. Norm Collins, personal correspondence with author, October 6, 1997
40. Mike and Gwen Byrne, personal correspondence with author, July 17, 1997
41. Barb Moldenhauer, personal correspondence with author, March 15, 1997
42. Vic Griffin, interview with author, November 1, 1996
43. Edwin Monk, "The Wedge," *Yachting*, January 1958, p.98
44. Edwin Monk, "Vancouver: the West Side Story," *SEA and Pacific Motorboat*, March 1965, p. 47
45. Edwin Monk, "A Vancouver Island Cruise," *Yachting*, December 1952, pp.41-42
46. Robert Gibson, personal correspondence with author, May 12, 1997
47. Robert P. Beebe, *Voyaging Under Power*, Seven Seas Press, New York, 1975, p.157
48. Ron Kondrat, personal correspondence with author, August 24, 1997
49. Tom Kincaid, personal correspondence with author, February 11, 1997

50. John West, personal correspondence with author, April 22, 1997
51. Robert P. Beebe, *Voyaging Under Power*, Seven Seas Press, New York, 1975, p.134
52. Robert P. Beebe, *Voyaging Under Power*, Seven Seas Press, New York, 1975, p.136
53. Robert P. Beebe, *Voyaging Under Power*, Seven Seas Press, New York, 1975, p.6
54. Edwin Monk, "A Designer Plans His Own Boat," *Yachting*, March 1956, p.63
55. "Naval Architect Edwin Monk Dies At Age 79," *Pacific Motor Boat,* March 1973
56. Edwin Monk, "Weight And The Motor Boat," *Yachting*, January 1955, p. 119
57. George McQueen, interview with author, October 22, 1996
58. Ibid.
59. Ed Monk Jr., interview with author, December 9, 1997
60. Graham Ross-Smith, personal correspondence with author, February 10, 1997
61. Fred Bailey, telephone conversation with author, November 4, 1997
62. Ed Monk Jr., interview with author, December 9, 1997
63. Susan MacDonald, personal correspondence with author, January 27, 1997
64. John Guzzwell, personal correspondence with author, November 22, 1997
65. Edwin Monk, "You And Your Naval Architect," *Yachting*, December 1963, p.41
66. Edwin Monk, "What Shape The Hull," *Yachting*, June 1969, p.70
67. Dave Gerr, *The Nature Of Boats*, International Marine Publishing, Camden, Maine, 1992, p.140
68. Robert Osborne, interview with author, February 14, 1997
69. L.H. "Mike" Michalson, personal correspondence with author, May 20, 1997
70. Judy Wade, personal correspondence with author, November 5, 1997
71. Ed Monk Jr., interview with author, December 9, 1997
72. Ian Kenning, personal correspondence with author, February 16, 1997
73. Edwin Monk, "Weight And The Motor Boat," *Yachting*, January 1955, p. 118
74. Edwin Monk, "Nika Sia," *SEA and Pacific Motor Boat*, February 1965, p.122
75. Edwin Monk, "Nika Sia," *SEA and Pacific Motor Boat*, February 1965, p.122
76. George McQueen, interview with author, October 22, 1996
77. Jim Dryburgh, interview with author, February 20, 1997
78. Ed Monk Jr., interview with author, December 9, 1997
79. Edwin Monk, "Monk Describes A New 50-Footer: His Own," *SEA and Pacific Motor Boat*, February 1971, p. 45
80. Judy Wade, personal correspondence with author, November 5, 1997
81. Edwin Monk, "Monk Describes A New 50-Footer: His Own," *SEA and Pacific Motor Boat*, February 1971, p.45

82. Larry and Colleen Price, personal correspondence with author, August 18, 1997
83. Norm Collins, personal correspondence with author, September 14, 1997
84. Norm Collins, personal correspondence with author, October 6, 1997
85. Judy Wade, personal correspondence with author, November 5, 1997
86. George McQueen, interview with author, October 22, 1996
87. Norm Collins, personal correspondence with author, October 6, 1996
88. Robert Gibson, personal correspondence with author, May 12, 1997
89. Harry Runer, personal correspondence with author, April 10, 1997
90. Bim Clark, personal correspondence with author, January 1, 1997
91. Warren Heard, interview with author, April 10, 1997

SOURCES

BOOKS
Beebe, Robert, *Voyaging Under Power*, Seven Seas Press, New York City, 1975
Beebe, Robert, *Voyaging Under Power*, Third Edition, revised by James F. Leishman, International Marine Publishing Company, Camden, Maine, 1994
Gerr, Dave, *The Nature Of Boats*, International Marine Publishing Company, Camden, Maine, 1992
Monk, Edwin, *Small Boat Building*, Charles Scribner's Sons, New York, 1934, revised 1947
Monk, Edwin, *Modern Boat Building*, Charles Scribner's Sons, New York, 1939, revised 1949
Newell, Gordon, *The H. W. McCurdy Marine History Of The Pacific Northwest*, Superior Publishing Company, Seattle, Washington, 1966

MAGAZINES
Northwest Yachting 1990 — 1997
Nor'westing 1970, 1989
Pacific Motor Boat 1929 — 1946
Pacific Yachting 1974 — 1997
Popular Boating 1962 — 1965
Sea 1983
SEA and Pacific Motor Boat 1965, 1971
Westcoast Fisherman 1990 — 1997
Westcoast Mariner 1995 — 1997
Western Fisheries 1952
WoodenBoat 1976 — 1997
Yachting 1933 — 1971

NEWSPAPERS AND JOURNALS
Bainbridge Review Vol. 73, No. 4
Marine Digest Vol. 36, No. 37
Seattle Times April 15, 1962; September 17, 1970
The Sea Chest March 1971

INDEX